EVER'S

MADNESS!

ET

W9-ABP-907

HONEYED APRICOT

HONEYED APRICOT

BUBBLE GUM

	STRAWBERRY	BERRY
STRAWBERRY		KEY LIME PIE
	CREAMSICLE	LEMONADE
HONEYED APRICOT		CREAMSICLE
	HONEYED APRICOT	PUMPKIN SPICE
HONEYED APRICOT		HONEYED APRICOT
	MARGARITA	BANANA
		MARGARITA
	CRÈME DE MENTHE	FUZZY NAVEL
CRÈME DE MENTHE		CRÈME DE MENTHE
	KOOL-AID	MALIBU
BUBBLE GUM		KOOL-AID
	BUBBLE GUM	BUBBLE GUM
BUBBLE GUM		MANGO CHILI LIME
	MAPLE BACON	MAPLE BACON
		PINEAPPLE ROSEMARY

MARSHMALLOW MADNESS!

Dozens of Puffalicious Recipes

by SHAUNA SEVER

photography by LEIGH BEISCH

Library of Congress Cataloging in Publication Number: 2011933440
ISBN: 978-1-59474-572-0
Printed in China
Design by Sugar
Photography by Leigh Beisch
Prop styling by Sara Slavin
Production management by John J. McGurk

Quirk Books
215 Church Street
Philadelphia, PA 19106
quirkbooks.com
10 9 8 7 6 5 4 3 2 1

CONTENTS

WAIT, YOU CAN MAKE MARSHMALLOWS?

Let's begin with a little story. A few years back, I was working on a television project for a show all about desserts and sweets. As a thank-you gift to the team, I made a whole mess of homemade marshmallows. The catch was that I had to fly to my destination and didn't want the marshmallows to get smooshed in my luggage, so I carried them onto the plane. As I passed through security, I was stopped and questioned about the contents of my cookie tins. When I informed the burly TSA agent they contained homemade marshmallows, I got some odd looks. A nervous flurry of questions filled my mind: Did I miss the news? Are they not allowing food through security this week? Do marshmallows count as gels? Oh, please don't make me toss my lovely sweet pillows from heaven! I was sure I was screwed.

But instead of scolding me for not knowing the rules, one of the agents said, "What? That's crazy, woman! You can't make marshmallows!" Relieved, I replied, "Oh, yes, sir. Oh, yes, you can!" and I offered him a sample. Chewing with enthusiastic approval, he waved me through the X-ray machine and murmured to his coworkers about my culinary ingenuity. True story.

My point is this: More than one person has looked at me like I was crazy when I said I was writing a book all about homemade marshmallows. People may look at you the same way when you first tell them you're making these sweet treats from scratch. But when you put a freshly made-from-scratch marshmallow in their face, you will come away the hero. Because there is simply nothing like homemade marshmallows—fluffy, soft, whipped pillows of sugar.

If all your marshmallow experiences have been limited to the sort that come out of plastic bags, prepare to have your world turned upside-down. You'll be shocked to learn that you, in fact, have never had a real marshmallow at all. And that you can create them in no time and then give them to other people and blow their minds, too. Hooray!

Like all great candymaking projects, mallow-making is equal parts confection and science experiment, a fantastic kitchen project, indeed. And there are endless flavor possibilities and ways to incorporate them in decadent desserts and creative crafting. Welcome to the crazy-sweet world of Marshmallow Madness!

INTRODUCTION

a sweet, sticky history of marshmallow

I'd wager that your idea of marshmallows is a lot like mine was for most of my life: They come in little plastic bags from the grocery store. You toast them around the campfire for s'mores, melt them for Rice Krispie treats, and drop the mini version in your hot cocoa in wintertime. And...that's pretty much the end of that story. Right? But in fact the history of the marshmallow is longer than the amount of time that bag of Jet-Puffed goodness will stay fresh in your cupboard.

Leave it to those amazing ancient Egyptians. They discovered how to extract the sticky, gelatinous sap from marshmallow root, which you can still find in health-food stores today. They combined the sap with honey to make a sticky confection, which was good for the sweet tooth as well as for medicinal purposes.

Westerners used the same basic concept to create an early version of the cough drop. Innovative nineteenth-century French candymakers further sweetened the formula and whipped air into the syrup to make a chewy confection. Extracting the sap was a laborious and expensive process, and soon the marshmallow-root part of the equation was abandoned in favor of gelatin (and sometimes an egg-white meringue as on page 24) to provide extra lift and stability.

American inventions like the extruder—the food-processing wonder that shapes just about every packaged food you can think of—made it easy to mass-produce what was once strictly an artisan confection. By the late 1940s, marshmallows had become the commercially available variety that we're all familiar with today.

In this book, we're gonna take you back to the Marshmallow Old School. Which is to say the fluffy, delicious French part. Not the ancient Egyptian cough drop part. Because that's just weird.

key marshmallow ingredients

For such a wow-inducing little treat, marshmallow requires just a handful of ingredients. Here are the essentials for whipping up a homemade batch of your very own.

SUGAR: A marshmallow without the sweet stuff is, well, definitely not a marshmallow. You'll need good white sugar and lots of it. I prefer working with pure cane sugar as opposed to generic beet sugar, because it's generally of higher quality and produces the most consistent results. All the recipes in this book that call for granulated sugar were tested with C&H Pure Cane Sugar. There's dozens of sugars on the market, and all are fair game for experimentation. If you want to play with "natural" sugars like turbinado or evaporated cane sugar (as in Mallows in the Raw, page 61), start by swapping out just a portion of the white sugar for the unrefined types.

CORN SYRUP: This essential ingredient keeps the sugar from crystallizing as you cook the syrup and adds to a good marshmallow's fluffy bounce and tender chew. There's a lot of debate about this product, particularly high-fructose corn syrup (HFCS). Many manufacturers (such as Karo) have reformulated their recipes so that their products do not include HFCS; check the label. I'm in the "everything in moderation" camp, so I like corn syrup for its consistent results and easy accessibility in supermarkets.

If you have allergies to corn syrup or just want to avoid it altogether, experiment with honey or other types of syrups, such as agave, maple, or brown rice; you'll find a few recipes in this book that incorporate these alternatives. You can also check the Web for recipes for homemade corn syrup substitutes. Your marshmallows may not come out exactly like those made with corn syrup, but they'll taste terrific, and you'll have a blast experimenting.

GELATIN: This is the magical ingredient that puffs up a marshmallow's structure and gives it an irresistible texture. As you whip the hot sugar syrup and gelatin together, the incorporated air cools the mixture and it sets into a light, pillowy mass. How much gelatin you use in a marshmallow recipe determines how firm and chewy your final result will be.

The kind of gelatin you use also matters. Gelatin comes in many forms, and the two most common are powder and sheets. I love working with sheets, but they can be tricky to find. So all the recipes in this book have been tested with Knox powdered gelatin, the most widely available unflavored gelatin (the kind that comes in little packets). Know that the amount of gelatin sold in packets can vary. Empty the contents into a measuring spoon according to the amount called for in the recipe to ensure you're using the right amount.

WATER: Yes, it sounds crazy, but since marshmallows contain only a few ingredients, you must make sure the water you're using tastes good. If your tap water is unsavory, use bottled water. You'll be glad you did.

GELATIN VS. EGG WHITES FOR PUFFING

There are two schools of thought on marshmallows. Most of the recipes in this book are based on gelatin and a sugar syrup. But other marshmallows are built on an egg-white meringue, like the Guimauve recipe on page 24. The gelatin-based type is my go-to mallow, since it's a bit sturdier and more versatile, you don't have to worry about food allergies, and it's safe for people avoiding raw egg whites. But egg-white-based mallows are fluffy, delicate little pieces of heaven, and they're definitely worth experimenting with.

Bump up the flavor of fruity marshmallows by using fruit nectars instead of water. Look for those that contain only fruit puree, water, and sugar—no high-fructose corn syrup.

SALT: Surprisingly important in confections, NaCl (sodium chloride) heightens flavors and balances sweetness, making everything more crave-worthy. I like to use a fine sea salt for its clean flavor, but table salt will work just as well.

VANILLA EXTRACT: The vast majority of the recipes in this book call for vanilla extract. Go for 100% pure for optimum flavor, and use the best you can find. To get fancy, you can add vanilla in the form of a scraped vanilla bean or an equal amount of vanilla bean paste.

COATING: Marshmallows need a light dusting of powder to keep them from sticking to everything in their path and to help the curing process. In this book, you'll see lots of ideas for marshmallow coatings. Here is my basic formula:

CLASSIC COATING

1 ½ cups confectioners' sugar
1 cup cornstarch or potato starch

Sift the ingredients together in a large bowl or combine them in a food processor. I tend to make several cups' worth at a time and store it in an airtight container; it keeps forever.

Classic Coating with nothing added will work on every recipe in this book. You can also use plain cornstarch or potato starch.

Coatings are a great way to add flavor and texture and to personalize your mallows. When the basic coating is made, scoop out what you need for a recipe and add a myriad of flavors using a whisk (or food processor for ingredients that need to be finely ground). You'll find that the recipes in this book call for either adding different spices or other ingredients into the coating or forgoing it in favor of coating with things like shredded toasted coconut, ground nuts, or graham cracker crumbs.

marshmallow tools

A few basic tools make all the difference—you don't need anything expensive or fancy. Here are a few pieces of common kitchen equipment that make mallowing easier and a lot more fun.

CANDY THERMOMETER: Consider it your brain while cooking sugar syrups—it does all the thinking for you. Just keep an eye on it, and when it reaches the temp indicated in the recipe, you're golden.

SAUCEPANS, SMALL AND LARGE: I use a few different sizes when making marshmallows. My beloved 1 ½-quart pot is so useful for the smaller amounts of syrup used in many recipes. Some recipes recommend a medium or large saucepan for syrups that tend to bubble up during boiling. The most important thing is not to use a pot so large that the level of the boiling syrup doesn't reach the candy thermometer.

MEASURING CUPS AND SPOONS: For measuring sugars and flours, I use dry measuring cups. For syrups, water, juices, and other liquids, I use liquid measures. It's the best way to ensure accuracy. A great tip for getting sticky things like corn syrup and honey to slip out of cups and spoons is to coat them first with a bit of nonstick cooking spray.

LET'S CALIBRATE!

Your thermometer must be calibrated to ensure accuracy. Candy thermometers are manufactured all over the world, so chances are slim that yours was made right at the altitude at which you live. Water boils at different temperatures depending on the altitude. I live at sea level in San Francisco, so that's 212°F, the baseline for boiling water. My sister lives in Denver, where her water boils at about 203°F. Ten degrees is an obvious difference, but, when cooking sugar, even five degrees can mean the difference between taffy and toffee.

It's easy to find out where you stand with your thermometer: Bring a small pot of water to a rapid, rolling boil. Clip your thermometer to the pan and give it 10 minutes to solidly register the temperature. That's your baseline. Whatever the difference is between that number and 212°F is what you'll need to add or subtract to arrive at the proper cooking temperatures indicated in these recipes. So that I don't forget, I write that difference in permanent ink on the thermometer, but I'm Type A like that.

Oh, and one other thing: Always, always make sure the tip of the thermometer is suspended in the syrup and not resting on the bottom of the blazing hot saucepan, which will wildly throw off the reading.

SMALL HEATPROOF WHISKS: Perfect for whisking your gelatin blooms and incorporating ingredients into hot syrups.

FLEXIBLE HEATPROOF SPATULAS: Indispensable in the marshmallowing kitchen, these are used to stir hot syrups and gelatin, scrape boiling syrup into the mixer bowl, fold ingredients into finished marshmallow batter, and scrape the whole lot of it cleanly into a prepared pan or mold.

STAND MIXER: For the most pleasant mallow-making experience, I recommend a heavy-duty electric stand mixer. Though not altogether impossible, making marshmallows is an awful lot of work for a hand mixer, and I know more than one person who has blown the motor. A stand mixer allows you to use both hands in the crucial first step of getting all the syrup into the mixer bowl. And for some recipes, like Homemade Marshmallow Crème (page 26), which gets extremely stiff, a stand mixer is the only workhorse up to the job.

8-BY-8-INCH PAN: Every marshmallow recipe included here will produce enough batter to fit nicely into this pan size. The slab can then be cut neatly into squares with **a pizza cutter** or **kitchen scissors** (also excellent marshmallow tools). But the 8-by-8 is just a guideline. You can pour the batter into any size or shape vessel or mold to make your mallows thicker or thinner; just make sure to coat it first with nonstick cooking spray. If you want to double any recipe, a 9-by-13-inch pan will work perfectly.

PIPING BAG AND PASTRY TIPS: These are awesome for cleanly depositing mallow batter into candy molds and piping all kinds of fun shapes. A large **zip-top bag** with one corner snipped off also works well for piping marshmallows.

For tips on how to make an explosion of pops, ropes, and twists like the ones on the cover, see "Tricks for Fancy Marshmallow Shapes" on page 41.

SMALL OFFSET SPATULA: The perfect tool for spreading and smoothing marshmallow batters into pans and leveling them into molds.

COOKING SPRAY: Marshmallows are sticky business. A light coating of nonstick cooking spray (canola oil based, unflavored is best) will save the day every time. Prepare your pans and molds with a light coating, and, if you really want everything to be nonstick, use it to lube your spatulas and scrapers. For a perfectly prepared mallow pan or mold, coat lightly with cooking spray and then use a paper towel or pastry brush to rub it all over the bottom and sides, removing excess and preventing beading or pooling in the pan.

TOOLS FOR COATING THE MARSHMALLOWS: Coating cured marshmallows with a powdered coating can be a royal mess, but there's a way to contain the chaos. When it's time to cut and coat your mallows, dump your powdered coating into a **large mixing bowl**. Have a similar-sized **sieve** standing by. Cut the marshmallow slab into squares (or whatever shapes you wish). Drop the mallows a few at a time into the mixing bowl full of coating and roll them around. Drop them into the sieve and shake it over the bowl to dust off excess coating, which will (hopefully) land in the bowl and not all over your counter.

GEL FOOD COLORINGS: Keep these highly concentrated tints on hand for all sorts of fun food projects. The bold hues mean that a little can go a long way, and because they're gels, not liquids, they won't upset the consistency of the marshmallow batter. Using food coloring is optional, of course, but I love the festive look just a few drops can add. And since I think food should look like what it tastes like, I often use a drop or two to bump up the color of the batter when using natural ingredients like fruit purees. When adding it to your batter, stop the mixer first so that the color doesn't spin all over the bowl.

A great online resource for every imaginable kitchen tool and ingredient is Culinary District (www.culinarydistrict.com). Here you can get everything you need for creative mallowing, from extracts to high-quality fruit purees, fancy sugars and cocoa powders, and gelatin in bulk, as well as cutters, molds, and piping tools.

marshmallow-making tips and techniques

As with all sugar work, the key to a fantastically enjoyable marshmallow-making experience is having everything ready before you start, and I mean *everything*. So read the recipe a couple times, and have all your tools within easy reach. Once that syrup has reached the right temp, it's go time! Hot sugar syrup waits for no one, so your gelatin must already be in the bowl with that blob of corn syrup and moving, waiting for the syrup to be drizzled in. Also, as soon as the mallow has been sufficiently whipped, it will immediately begin to set, so get it scraped into your prepared pan (or piped into your molds) and smoothed right quick, while it's workable.

You can expect your first batch of marshmallow batter to come together in about 30 minutes, including prep time; that time will decrease as you get the hang of the process. The marshmallow will need to set for at least six hours; recommendations for curing times are included with each recipe.

All the recipes in this book will come together in more or less the same way. Here's a run-down of what should happen in each step. Refer to this section if you find yourself needing tips or visual cues while engaging in sweet, sweet mallow-making.

"Blooming" gelatin refers to softening it in a liquid before using it in a recipe. Prepare your bloom nice and early to ensure it's fully hydrated. First, put your cold water or other liquids in a small heatproof bowl; then sprinkle the gelatin over it before whisking. You'll get fewer lumps this way.

I recommend 5 to 10 minutes of blooming time, but there's no such thing as letting a bloom go too long—more time is always better than not enough. When I'm ready to deal with the bloomed gelatin, I melt it with a quick 20- to 30-second zap in the microwave (or over simmering water in a double boiler, if you're micro-less) and then give it a good whisking. Finally, I rub a bit of the mixture between my fingers to make sure there are no undisolved granules before adding the bloom to the mixer bowl.

The base for all the recipes in this book is a mixture of sugar, corn syrup, water, and a touch of salt, melted to a syrup and then boiled to a certain temperature. Sometimes I'll throw in additional liquids, depending on the flavor. Whatever is in the syrup pot is what you'll stir together gently over high heat. When the sugar has dissolved and the syrup comes up to a bubble, clip a candy thermometer onto the pan. From there, just keep a keen eye on that temperature until it reaches the degree indicated in the recipe. You can also stir the mixture occasionally if you wish or if the recipe calls for it to prevent burning.

In this step, the bloomed gelatin, hot sugar syrup, and air come together with the help of an electric mixer…and pure, pillowy magic happens. I never tire of watching fresh marshmallow billowing up in my mixer bowl. At this stage, you might add extra flavorings to the batter, and you'll pour or pipe it into a waiting pan or molds and dust it with a coating before letting it cure.

You might notice that my method for marshmallow-making is different from most. Many other similar recipes have you whisking the bloom into the hot syrup and then pouring the whole lot into a running stand mixer on high speed. I've done it this way, and you tend to get a whole lot of sugar syrup spinning onto the sides of the bowl rather than into your mallow batter, along with a good chance of ending up in a burn unit. Not delicious, really dangerous.

What I like to do instead is divide the measure of corn syrup, putting half in my mixer bowl and half in the pot. My melted bloom then goes into the corn syrup in the mixer bowl, and, by the time the hot sugar syrup goes in, there's already a nice amount of viscous goo in the bowl to catch the hot liquid and keep it from flying onto my kitchen ceiling. This is also a good time to note how extremely dangerous hot sugar syrup can be. Sugar heats up a heck of a lot hotter than boiling water, and if you get some on your skin, it sticks immediately and keeps on burning. So be careful not to get too close while heating your syrup, and wear an oven mitt as you pour the syrup into the mixer bowl, standing back a bit while doing so. Use the beating times and mixer speeds in the recipes to help determine when the marshmallow batter is sufficiently whipped. Using the levels of a 10-speed stand mixer as examples, here's a reference guide to the speeds I suggest in these recipes:

LOW SPEED	MEDIUM SPEED	MEDIUM-HIGH SPEED	HIGH SPEED
=	=	=	=
2	5 TO 6	8	10

If you don't whip the batter enough, you'll get dense, heavy mallows. Too much whipping and the gelatin will have already set, and you won't be able to get it into the pan and spread it smoothly. A well-whipped batter will have begun billowing up in the bowl and climbing the whip. When you stop the mixer, the batter should slump down the whip attachment ever so slightly, but not look runny. If you pull the whisk out of the batter, it should hold a soft shape. The humidity and temperature in the room will affect how quickly this happens, so keep that in mind as you check for doneness. After a couple batches of marshmallows, you'll absolutely be able to eye a batter and know when it's whipped correctly.

Now, before you start thinking that mallow-making is some kind of military operation and you'll need a nap and a stiff drink afterward, just remember this: Getting everything together and being familiar with the process before you start make malloweing easier and a lot more fun. And, ultimately, fun is what we're after here. Because, really, what's happier and more fun than marshmallow?

PUFF PIECE: STORING YOUR MALLOWS

The best conditions for mallow-making and storage (or for any kind of sugar work, really) are cool and dry. During the curing process, the marshmallow needs to dry out to maintain its optimum texture, which is nearly impossible in humid or rainy weather. The best situation for curing and storing marshmallows is one in which they stay as dry as possible. Your fridge might seem like a logical choice, but often it can harbor lots of moisture. The countertop is usually a better option.

After spreading the batter into your pan or molds and dusting with plenty of coating, cure the mallow uncovered. Store the cut mallows in single layers in a covered container, with one corner cracked to allow for a little air flow. (If the weather calls for extra-dry insurance, add a sheet of paper toweling dusted with coating between each layer.) You'll find that some flavors tend to resist drying more than others (notably, fruit flavors), but no worries. Worst-case scenario: Dust more coating on any mallows that have become damp on the outside and set them uncovered on a sheet tray to dry again before packaging or storing. I'll give you a heads-up at the end of a recipe if a particular flavor usually needs to be redusted with coating after a day or two of storage.

ACKNOWLEDGMENTS

Thank you to the fantastically creative and enthusiastic team at Quirk Books who made this book a reality, especially my tirelessly supportive editor, Margaret McGuire. Thank you to Alexis Soterakis for helping me wade through my first book contract. Enormous, beautifully lit thanks to the whole crew at Leigh Beisch Photography and to prop-stylist extraordinaire Sara Slavin. Much gratitude to Dave for his vegan marshmallow inspiration and to Rosie Alyea for introducing me to an early version of Blonde Rocky Road. Virtual hugs to the wonderful readers of my blog "Piece of Cake"; Sara, Erin, Lauren, Christina, and Steph for being a constant source of personal support; my wonderful family, especially Mom and Tiff, for always being there for me and pushing me forward with your love. And to my darling Scott and Caroline, for tasting way more marshmallows than any human being should ever ingest—you two are the sweetest things in my life.

THE CLASSICS

Vanilla and Chocolate Marshmallows

What better way to kick off the sweet, fluffy party than with a nod to the timeless flavors of vanilla and chocolate? Learning to whip up a perfect vanilla mallow will be your launching pad to endless possibilities of add-ins and flavorings—it's the ultimate blank canvas for all sorts of confection creativity. And everybody knows that where there's vanilla, there's got to be chocolate. It's just the right thing to do.

CLASSIC VANILLA MARSHMALLOWS

About 2 dozen 1 ½-inch mallows

Lightly coat an 8-by-8-inch baking pan with cooking spray.

WHISK TOGETHER the gelatin and cold water in a small bowl and let soften for 5 minutes.

STIR TOGETHER the sugar, ¼ cup of the corn syrup, water, and salt in a medium saucepan over high heat. Boil, stirring occasionally, until the temperature reaches 240°F. Meanwhile, pour remaining ¼ cup corn syrup into the bowl of an electric mixer fitted with the whisk attachment. Microwave gelatin on high until completely melted, about 30 seconds. Pour it into the mixer bowl. Set the mixer speed to low and keep it running.

WHEN THE SYRUP reaches 240°F, slowly pour it into the mixer bowl. Increase the speed to medium and beat for 5 minutes. Increase to medium-high and beat for 5 more minutes. Beat on the highest setting for 1 to 2 minutes more and beat in the vanilla; the finished marshmallow will be opaque white, fluffy, and tripled in volume. Pour it into the prepared pan, using an offset spatula to smooth it into the corners. Sift coating evenly and generously over top. Let set for at least 6 hours in a cool, dry place.

Use a knife to loosen the marshmallow from the edges of the pan. Invert the slab onto a coating-dusted work surface and dust it with more coating. Cut into whatever size pieces you wish (a pizza cutter works great for squares). Dip the sticky edges of the marshmallows in more coating, patting off the excess.

Super vanilla-ize these mallows by adding a scraped vanilla bean or dab of pure vanilla bean paste along with the vanilla extract (see vanilla extract entry in "Key Ingredients," page 8).

the bloom
- 4 ½ teaspoons unflavored powdered gelatin
- ½ cup cold water

the syrup
- ¾ cup sugar
- ½ cup light corn syrup, divided
- ¼ cup water
- ⅛ teaspoon salt

the mallowing
- 2 teaspoons pure vanilla extract
- ½ cup Classic Coating (page 8), plus more for dusting

MORE MALLOWS

Chocolate Chip Marshmallows: Fold in ½ cup mini semisweet chocolate chips before pouring the marshmallow into the prepared pan.

Torrone Marshmallows: Substitute 2 tablespoons honey for half the corn syrup in the Syrup stage. Fold ⅓ cup toasted, chopped salted pistachios and ¼ cup dried, sweetened cranberries into the fully whipped batter.

Cookies 'n Cream Marshmallows: Fold ⅓ cup crushed Oreo cookies into the beaten marshmallow batter. Take it a step further by rolling the finished cut mallows in crushed cookies instead of Classic Coating.

HOMEMADE MINI MARSHMALLOWS

These are super simple and way too easy to nibble on by the handful. Line a large baking sheet with parchment paper and dust it generously with Classic Coating (page 8). Make a batch of Classic Vanilla Marshmallows, but omit the last minute of beating on high speed, instead adding the vanilla during the last minute of medium-high beating. Load the batter into a large pastry bag fitted with a large round pastry tip (or use a disposable zip-top plastic bag with one corner snipped off). Pipe long lines of marshmallow in parallel rows across the baking sheet. Dust with more coating and let cure. When set, use kitchen scissors to snip the marshmallow sticks into ½-inch-wide bits. Roll the mini mallows in the coating right on the baking sheet, dusting off the excess.

DEEPLY CHOCOLATE MARSHMALLOWS

About 2 dozen 1 ½-inch mallows

Lightly coat an 8-by-8-inch baking pan with cooking spray.

WHISK TOGETHER the gelatin and cold water in a small bowl. Let it soften for 5 minutes.

MAKE THE CHOCOLATE SYRUP: In the bowl of an electric mixer, whisk together the cocoa powder, espresso powder, and hot water until smooth. Whisk in corn syrup.

STIR TOGETHER the sugar, remaining ¼ cup corn syrup, water, and salt in a medium saucepan over high heat. Boil, stirring occasionally, until it hits 248°F to 250°F. Microwave the gelatin on high until completely melted, about 30 seconds. Pour it into the chocolate syrup. Set your mixer to low and keep it running.

WHEN THE SYRUP reaches 248°F to 250°F, slowly pour it into the mixer bowl. Increase the speed to medium and beat for 5 minutes. Increase to medium-high and beat for 5 more minutes. Increase to the highest setting and beat for 3 to 5 minutes more, adding vanilla in the last minute. The finished marshmallow will be tripled in volume. Pour it into the prepared pan, using an offset spatula to smooth it into the corners. Sift coating evenly over top. Let set for about 6 hours in a cool, dry place.

Use a knife to loosen the marshmallow from the edges of the pan. Invert the slab onto a coating-dusted work surface and dust with more coating. Cut it into pieces and dip the sticky edges in more coating, patting off the excess.

MORE MALLOWS

Chocolate-Peppermint Marshmallows: Simply add ½ teaspoon pure peppermint extract along with the vanilla.

Mocha Marshmallows: In both the Bloom and Chocolate Syrup, swap out the plain water for brewed coffee: cold coffee for the Bloom, and hot for the Chocolate Syrup.

the bloom
- 5 teaspoons unflavored powdered gelatin
- ½ cup cold water

the chocolate syrup
- 3 tablespoons dark unsweetened cocoa powder*
- ¾ teaspoon instant espresso powder**
- ¼ cup hot water
- ¼ cup light corn syrup

the sugar syrup
- 1 cup sugar
- ¼ cup light corn syrup
- ¼ cup water
- ¼ teaspoon salt

the mallowing
- 1 teaspoon pure vanilla extract
- ½ cup Classic Coating (page 8), whisked with 1 tablespoon cocoa powder

Buy the darkest cocoa powder you can find. Good quality really makes a difference in this recipe. I live for Valrhona cocoa powder.

**If you can't find instant espresso powder, replace with 1 ½ teaspoons instant coffee granules. Coffee greatly heightens the chocolate flavor.*

CHOCOLATE-FILLED VANILLA MARSHMALLOWS

About 3 dozen 1 ½-inch mallows

Lightly coat 36 wells of mini-muffin tins with cooking spray. Fit a large pastry bag with a large round tip. Have ready a small plastic pastry or zip-top bag and a pair of scissors.

PREPARE A BATCH of Classic Vanilla Marshmallows. During the beating stage, beat the batter on medium speed for 5 minutes and then increase to medium-high and beat for 5 minutes more, beating in the vanilla during the last minute. You want the marshmallow batter to be just slightly warm to the touch, somewhat fluid, and barely holding a soft peak.

MAKE THE GANACHE: While the marshmallow is beating, place the chocolate and cream in a small heatproof bowl. Microwave on high for 20 to 25 seconds. Stir until the chocolate is melted and the mixture is smooth. Load the ganache into the small pastry bag and set aside. (If using a zip-top bag, snip a small corner off the bag before piping.) Quickly scrape beaten marshmallow into the large pastry bag. Pipe the batter into the wells of the mini-muffin tins, filling them only halfway. Pipe a dab (about ¼ teaspoon) of ganache in the center of each marshmallow. Immediately pipe the remainder of the marshmallow batter into tins, covering the ganache and filling the wells to the tops. Sift coating evenly over top. Let set for at least 4 hours.

Use the tip of a small knife to loosen and remove the marshmallows from the tins and immediately roll them in coating, patting off the excess.

These filled marshmallows are pure magic. Beating the marshmallow a few minutes shy of its normal whipping time keeps the batter softer and more fluid and allows it to completely envelop a bittersweet chocolate ganache. Everyone will think you're a genius and wonder how you did it.

Continued...

the mallowing

- 1 batch Classic Vanilla Marshmallows (page 16)
- ½ cup Classic Coating (page 8), plus more for dusting

the ganache filling

- 2 ounces bittersweet chocolate (60% to 70% cacao), chopped
- 1 ounce (2 tablespoons) heavy cream

MORE MALLOWS

Kahlua-Filled Marshmallows: Make a batch of Mocha Marshmallows, omitting the last minute of beating time before transferring the batter to the pastry bag. Flavor the ganache with a couple teaspoons of Kahlua (or any liqueur you love).

Jam-Filled Marshmallows: Use about ⅓ cup low-sugar jam or jelly as the filling. For a double punch of fruit flavor, make a corresponding flavored marshmallow batter to pair with the filling.

Rose-Filled Marshmallows: Replace the bittersweet chocolate in the ganache with an equal amount of chopped white chocolate. Stir in a drop of rose oil or several drops of rose water, to taste. Tint the ganache with pink food coloring. You can also use fruit-flavored extracts in place of the rose flavoring.

Candy Bar Marshmallow Bites: Tuck a hunk of your favorite candy bar into the mallow batter before topping it off.

Using a piping bag makes it easy to cleanly deposit marshmallow batter into small candy molds.

CHOCOLATE MALT MARSHMALLOWS

About 2 dozen 1 ½-inch mallows

Lightly coat an 8-by-8-inch baking pan with cooking spray.

WHISK TOGETHER the gelatin and cold water in a small bowl, and let it soften for 5 minutes.

MAKE THE CHOCOLATE MALT SYRUP: In the bowl of an electric mixer, whisk together the cocoa powder, malted milk powder, hot water, and corn syrup until smooth. Put the bowl on the mixer and fit it with the whisk attachment.

STIR TOGETHER the sugar, corn syrup, water, and salt in a medium saucepan over high heat. Boil, stirring occasionally, until the temperature reaches 248°F to 250°F. Meanwhile, microwave the gelatin on high until completely melted, about 30 seconds, and pour it into the chocolate syrup. Set the mixer to low and keep it running while you check the sugar syrup.

WHEN THE SYRUP reaches 248°F to 250°F, slowly pour it into the mixer bowl. Increase the speed to medium and beat for 5 minutes. Increase to medium-high and beat for 5 more minutes. Increase to the highest setting and beat for 3 to 5 minutes more, adding the vanilla in the last minute. The finished marshmallow will be tripled in volume. Pour it into the prepared pan, using an offset spatula to smooth it into the corners. Sprinkle grated chocolate evenly and generously over top. Let set for about 6 hours.

Use a knife to loosen the marshmallow from the edges of the pan and invert the slab onto a work surface. Sprinkle it with grated chocolate. Cut it into pieces and dip the sticky edges in more chocolate, patting off the excess.

To shave the chocolate, grate bar chocolate over the largest holes of a box grater.

the bloom
- 5 teaspoons unflavored powdered gelatin
- ½ cup cold water

the chocolate malt syrup
- 3 tablespoons dark unsweetened cocoa powder*
- ½ cup plain malted milk powder**
- 7 tablespoons hot water
- ¼ cup light corn syrup

the sugar syrup
- 1 cup sugar
- ¼ cup light corn syrup
- ¼ cup water
- ¼ teaspoon salt

the mallowing
- 1 teaspoon pure vanilla extract
- ⅔ cup grated bittersweet chocolate (60% to 70% cacao)

* The deeper and richer the cocoa powder, the more intense the color and flavor will be (I like Valrhona).

** Look for plain malted milk powder (not the chocolate-flavored kind) in supermarkets, either near the hot cocoa mixes or by the ice-cream fixings. Carnation and Horlicks are popular brands.

GUIMAUVE

About 2 dozen 1 ½-inch mallows

Lightly coat an 8-by-8-inch baking pan with cooking spray.

🌑 **WHISK TOGETHER** the gelatin and cold water in a small bowl and let it soften for 5 minutes.

🌑 **MAKE THE MERINGUE:** Place the egg whites in the bowl of an electric mixer fitted with the whisk attachment. Whip on medium-high speed until they are opaque white and just begin to hold soft peaks, 2 to 3 minutes.

🌑 **STIR TOGETHER** the sugar, corn syrup, water, and salt in a medium saucepan over high heat. Boil, stirring occasionally, until the temperature reaches 240°F.

🌑 **WHEN THE SYRUP** reaches 240°F, start the mixer on medium-high speed. Quickly whisk the bloomed gelatin into the syrup until melted. With the mixer running, carefully drizzle just a few tablespoons of syrup into the egg whites—you want to slowly warm the eggs to avoid scrambling them. Repeat 2 or 3 more times with a few more drizzles of syrup and then pour in the rest, using a heatproof spatula to ensure all the syrup is scraped into the mixer bowl. Beat on medium-high speed for 5 minutes. Increase to high and beat for 5 to 7 minutes more, adding the vanilla in the last minute.

The finished marshmallow will be tripled in volume. Pour it into the prepared pan, using an offset spatula to smooth it into the corners. Sift coating evenly over top. Let it set for 6 hours in a cool, dry place. Use a knife to loosen the marshmallow from the edges of the pan. Invert the slab onto a coating-dusted work surface and dust with more coating. Cut it into pieces and dip the sticky edges in more coating, patting off the excess.

Pâte de guimauve is the gloriously French way of saying "marshmallow." So, in keeping with our mallow nickname here, we'll just go with guimauve. D'accord?

🌑 **the bloom**
4 ½ teaspoons unflavored powdered gelatin
½ cup cold water

🌑 **the meringue**
2 large egg whites, at room temperature

🌑 **the syrup**
1 cup granulated sugar
½ cup corn syrup
¼ cup water
⅛ teaspoon salt

🌑 **the mallowing**
2 teaspoons pure vanilla extract*
½ cup Classic Coating (page 8), plus more for dusting

* I love these marshmallows best with just a breath of vanilla in the form of extract or a scraped bean. But you can easily incorporate other flavors by using different liquids in the bloom and whipping in extracts at the end of beating.

VEGAN VANILLA MARSHMALLOWS

About 2 dozen 1 1/2-inch mallows

Along with the Genutine, this mallow's structure and lightness comes from a sort of soy "fluff" that mimics an egg-white meringue. Even if you're not vegan, it's good fun seeking out a few exotic ingredients and taking an adventure into molecular gastronomy to whip up these little pillows of heaven. This marshmallow-making process is different—and it doesn't require the use of a candy thermometer!

Lightly coat an 8-by-8-inch baking pan with cooking spray.

◆ **MAKE THE FLUFF:** In the bowl of a stand mixer, whisk together all ingredients until smooth. Put the bowl on the mixer and fit it with the whisk attachment. Beat the fluff on high speed until it triples in volume and forms firm peaks, about 7 to 8 minutes (it will resemble softly whipped cream). Stop the mixer.

◆ **PLACE THE SUGAR,** Genutine, corn syrup, water, and salt in a food processor and process for 1 minute. Pour the syrup into a large saucepan and stir gently over high heat. Boil for 8 minutes, stirring often. The syrup will thicken, forming bubbles almost 1 inch in diameter; you should see flashes of the bottom of the pan as you stir. Stir in the vanilla.

◆ **RESTART THE MIXER** on medium speed. Quickly scrape the syrup into the mixer bowl all at once and immediately increase the speed to high. Beat for 7 to 9 minutes on high speed; the candy will turn opaque white and fluffy, and nearly fill the bowl. Scrape it into the prepared pan. Place a large sheet of parchment paper spritzed with cooking spray on top and use both hands to smooth the marshmallow evenly into the corners. Let set at room temperature for 4 to 6 hours.

Remove parchment and use a knife to loosen the marshmallow from the edges of the pan. Invert the slab onto a coating-dusted work surface and dust it with more coating. Cut into pieces and dip the sticky edges in more coating, patting off the excess.

Extracts and candy oils are your best bet for flavoring vegan mallows any way you like.

◆ **the fluff**
- 1/3 cup unflavored soy protein isolate 90%*
- 2 teaspoons baking powder
- 1/4 teaspoon xantham gum
- 2/3 cup water

◆ **the syrup**
- 1 1/2 cups sugar
- 1 tablespoon Genutine*
- 1 cup light corn syrup
- 1/2 cup water
- 1/4 teaspoon salt
- 2 teaspoons pure vanilla extract

◆ **the mallowing**
- 1/2 cup Classic Coating (page 8), plus more for dusting

* Readily available at natural-food stores; make sure the label reads 90%.

* Genutine is a vegetable gelatin that is available online (visit Le-sanctuaire.com).

HOMEMADE MARSHMALLOW CRÈME

About 2 ½ cups

● **STIR TOGETHER** the sugar, light corn syrup, water, and salt in a small saucepan over high heat. Boil, stirring occasionally, until it reaches 240°F.

● **PLACE THE EGG WHITES** and cream of tartar in the bowl of an electric mixer fitted with the whisk attachment. Start whipping the egg whites to soft peaks on medium speed.

The goal is to have the egg whites whipped and ready, waiting for your syrup to be drizzled in. If they're whipping faster than your syrup is coming to temperature, just stop the mixer until the syrup is ready.

● **WHEN THE SYRUP** reaches 240°F, set the mixer to low and slowly drizzle a tiny bit of syrup, a couple tablespoons' worth, into the egg whites to warm them. (If you add too much syrup at once, the whites will scramble.) Slowly drizzle in the rest of the syrup and then increase the speed to medium-high. Beat until the marshmallow crème is stiff and glossy, 7 to 9 minutes; toward the end of the beating time, beat in the vanilla. Use immediately or store in an airtight container in the refrigerator for up to 2 weeks.

I simply cannot put into words how glorious this fluffy homemade marshmallow crème is. You can use it as an ice-cream topping, whoopie-pie filling, or cake frosting. You can beat in some butter to make it a richer filling, as in the Chocolate-Marshmallow Roulade (page 87). It's just the sort of thing that makes you smack yourself and say, "Why have I not been doing this my entire life?" It really is that spectacular.

● the syrup
- ¾ cup sugar
- ½ cup light corn syrup
- ¼ cup water
- ⅛ teaspoon salt

● the fluff
- 2 large egg whites, at room temperature
- ¼ teaspoon cream of tartar

● the mallowing
- 1 ½ teaspoons pure vanilla extract*

* Using small amounts of extracts, essential oils, and candy oils is the best and easiest way to flavor homemade fluff.

HOMEMADE GRAHAM CRACKERS

When it comes to sweet-treat pairings, marshmallows and graham crackers go together like Oprah and Gayle. For the ultimate from-scratch s'mores, whip up some of these homemade wafers and sandwich them with your favorite mallow flavor. Or crush them to create next-level crumbs for pie crusts and other recipes (like S'mores Cupcakes, page 85).

GRAHAM CRACKERS

About 4 dozen 2 ½-inch crackers

- 2 cups all-purpose flour
- ½ cup stone-ground whole wheat flour
- ½ cup packed dark brown sugar
- 1 teaspoon salt
- ½ teaspoon ground cinnamon
- 1 cup unsalted butter, cut into small pieces
- ¼ cup honey
  Turbinado sugar, for sprinkling (optional)

In the bowl of a food processor, blend together the all-purpose flour, whole wheat flour, brown sugar, salt, and cinnamon. Add the butter pieces and the honey and blend until the mixture comes together. Scrape out the dough onto a sheet of plastic wrap and pat it into a rectangular shape; wrap well. Refrigerate until firm but still pliable, about 1 hour.

Position an oven rack in the center position and preheat to 350°F. Line two baking sheets with parchment paper or silicone baking mats. Turn out the dough onto a lightly floured surface and roll out thinly, about ⅛ inch thick (you can gather the dough scraps and reroll as necessary). Cut out crackers with a 2- to 3-inch cookie cutter (or cut into squares with a pizza cutter) and place pieces on the prepared baking sheets, a dozen per sheet. Prick each one several times with a fork and sprinkle with turbinado sugar, if desired. Chill the pieces on the sheets for at least 15 minutes before baking. Bake for 14 to 16 minutes until golden. Let set for 1 minute before transferring the crackers to a rack to cool completely.

VEGAN, GLUTEN-FREE GRAHAM CRACKERS

About 4 dozen 2 ½-inch crackers

- 2 ¼ cups gluten-free all-purpose flour mix*
- ½ cup firmly packed dark brown sugar
- 1 ¼ teaspoons ground cinnamon
- 1 teaspoon baking powder
- ½ teaspoon baking soda
- ½ teaspoon xanthan gum
- ½ teaspoon salt
- 7 tablespoons margarine or nondairy butter substitute, cut into pieces**
- ¼ cup cold water
- 3 tablespoons honey (or agave nectar)
- 1 teaspoon pure vanilla extract

I like Bob's Red Mill all-purpose gluten-free flour blend, available at most supermarkets.

**I use Earth Balance sticks for this recipe.*

In the bowl of a food processor, blend together the flour mix, brown sugar, cinnamon, baking powder, baking soda, xanthan gum, and salt. Pulse in the margarine until the mixture resembles coarse crumbs. Add the water, honey, and vanilla and blend until the mixture comes together in a ball. Turn out the dough onto a sheet of plastic wrap and pat it into a rectangular shape; wrap tightly and refrigerate for at least 1 hour.

Preheat the oven to 325°F. Line two baking sheets with parchment paper or silicone baking mats. Roll out the dough to a large rectangle about ⅛ inch thick. Use a pizza cutter to cut it into squares. Transfer the squares to the prepared baking sheets and freeze until firm, about 5 minutes. Prick each piece several times with a fork. Bake until firm and golden brown, 16 to 18 minutes. Let cool for 1 minute on the sheet pans before transferring the crackers to a wire rack to cool completely.

FRESH AND FRUITY

Adding Twists of Flavor with Fruit Purees, Juices, and Oils

Vanilla marshmallows are mind-blowing in their tender, puffy sweetness. But start dabbling in fruit-flavored varieties, and people will nominate you for some kind of award. The best part is, there are oh-so many ways to incorporate fruit flavors into marshmallows. In this section, you'll learn a few techniques that'll have you dreaming up your own flavors in no time. Here's where we play with fruit juices, nectars, concentrates, purees, essential oils, and—get this—baby food. Now the real mallowing fun begins.

CONCORD GRAPE MARSHMALLOWS
About 2 dozen 1 ½-inch mallows

Lightly coat 2 dozen dome-shaped candy molds or an 8-by-8-inch baking pan with cooking spray.

🌸 **WHISK TOGETHER** the gelatin, Concord grape concentrate, and cold water in a small bowl. Let it soften for 10 minutes.

💧 **STIR TOGETHER** the sugar, ¼ cup of the corn syrup, water, and salt in a medium saucepan. Bring the syrup to a boil over high heat and stir occasionally until it hits 250°F. Pour the remaining ¼ cup corn syrup into the bowl of an electric mixer fitted with the whisk attachment. Microwave the gelatin on high until melted, about 30 seconds, and pour it into the corn syrup. Set the mixer to low and keep it running.

🌸 **WHEN THE SYRUP** reaches 250°F, slowly pour it into the mixer bowl. Increase the speed to medium and beat for 5 minutes. Increase to medium-high and beat for 3 more minutes. Beat on the highest setting for 1 to 2 minutes more, adding the vanilla during the last minute. The finished marshmallow will be tripled in volume.

Load the batter into a large pastry bag fitted with a large round tip. Pipe the batter into the wells of the prepared candy molds (or scrape batter into the prepared 8-by-8-inch pan). Sift coating over the top. Let set for 8 hours in a cool, dry place.

Gently nudge the set marshmallows out of the molds and roll in coating, sifting off the excess.

Layer a batch of Concord Grape with Fluffernutter Marshmallow to make a killer PB&J confection (page 68).

MORE MALLOWS

Apple-Cinnamon Marshmallows: Swap out the grape concentrate for unsweetened apple juice concentrate. Cook the syrup to 240°F. During the Mallowing stage, beat in ½ teaspoon of ground cinnamon. (Try Vietnamese cinnamon for an extra kick.)

🌸 the bloom
- 4 ½ teaspoons unflavored powdered gelatin
- ½ cup unsweetened Concord grape concentrate,* thawed but still cold
- ¼ cup cold water

💧 the syrup
- ¾ cup sugar
- ½ cup light corn syrup, divided
- ¼ cup water
- ¼ teaspoon salt

🌸 the mallowing
- 1 teaspoon pure vanilla extract
- ½ cup Classic Coating (page 8), plus more for dusting

* Welch's makes a great, inexpensive Concord grape concentrate that's widely available in supermarkets. You can also use intensely flavored fruit purees and concentrates from companies like Boiron or the Perfect Puree of Napa Valley.

STRAWBERRY MARSHMALLOWS

About 2 dozen 1 ½-inch mallows

Lightly coat an 8-by-8-inch baking pan with cooking spray.

WHISK TOGETHER the strawberry puree and water in a small heatproof bowl. Whisk in the gelatin and let it soften for 10 minutes.

STIR TOGETHER the sugar, ¼ cup of the corn syrup, strawberry puree, water, and salt in a large saucepan over high heat. Boil until it reaches 240°F; while the syrup is cooking, use a rigid heatproof spatula to stir occasionally, scraping the bottom of the pan to keep the syrup from burning. This syrup has a tendency to boil up high in the pan, so be prepared to adjust the heat to prevent it from bubbling over. Meanwhile, pour the remaining ¼ cup corn syrup into the bowl of an electric mixer fitted with the whisk attachment. Microwave the gelatin on high until completely melted, about 30 seconds. Pour it into the corn syrup. Set the mixer to low and keep it running.

WHEN THE SYRUP reaches 240°F, slowly pour it into the mixer bowl. If any syrup has burned on the bottom of the pan, don't fret—just don't scrape any into the batter. Increase the speed to medium and beat for 5 minutes. Increase to medium-high and beat for 5 to 7 more minutes, adding the vanilla in the last minute. The finished marshmallow will be tripled in volume. Fold in the freeze-dried strawberries. Pour it into the prepared pan, using an offset spatula to smooth it into the corners. Sift the coating generously over top. Let it set for at least 8 hours.

Use a knife to loosen the marshmallow from the edges of the pan. Invert the slab onto a coating-dusted work surface and dust it with more coating. Cut it into pieces and dip the sticky edges in more coating, patting off the excess.

MORE MALLOWS

Raspberry or Blackberry Marshmallows: Get a radically different flavor by swapping out the strawberry puree in both the Bloom and Syrup stages with an equal amount of strained raspberry or blackberry puree. You can also find freeze-dried versions of these berries.

the bloom
- ½ cup strained strawberry puree*
- 2 tablespoons cold water
- 2 tablespoons unflavored powdered gelatin

the syrup
- ¾ cup sugar
- ½ cup light corn syrup, divided
- ⅓ cup strained strawberry puree
- ¼ cup water
- ⅛ teaspoon salt

the mallowing
- 1 teaspoon pure vanilla extract
- ½ cup freeze-dried strawberries*
- ½ cup Classic Coating (page 8), plus more for dusting

If seeds bug you, take the extra step and strain the puree through a fine-mesh sieve. One 10-ounce bag of frozen berries will yield enough strained puree for these marshmallows.

Find these firm, brittle, flavor-packed gems at natural-food stores under the brand name "Just Strawberries." Throwing a small handful into a food processor with Classic Coating makes for a pretty pink color.

KEEPING IT REAL WITH NATURAL FRUIT FLAVORS

When dealing with a confection that consists primarily of sugar and corn syrup, nutrition isn't exactly a concern. But that shouldn't stop us from using otherwise healthful ingredients, like real fruit, in these sweet delights. A fresh marshmallow flavored with real fruit is truly delicious, especially when the fruits are at their peak.

Some of the best and boldest flavors come from pureeing the fruit (as opposed to just using the juice). For berry flavors, simply place clean fresh or thawed frozen berries in a food processor and puree until smooth; run the puree through a mesh sieve to remove the seeds, if desired.

Peel stone fruits like peaches and plums before pureeing. Here's a quick tip for removing skins: Cut a small X in the bottom of each fruit and drop them into a pot of boiling water for about 30 seconds. Transfer to a big bowl of ice water to cool them down quickly. When cool enough to handle, the skins should slip right off. You can also puree thawed frozen stone fruits (or any fruit, for that matter); just make sure to buy them unsweetened.

Fruit juice concentrates that are free of added sugars are easy to find in supermarkets and provide intense flavor and color (as in the Concord Grape and Apple-Cinnamon marshmallows, page 30). To experiment with more exotic fruit flavors like pomegranate, lychee, and passion fruit, opt for higher-end fruit concentrates and finely strained purees (Boiron and the Perfect Puree of Napa Valley are two to try).

And, last but not least, baby food! The genius of using fruit baby foods in marshmallows is three-fold: First, all the prep work has been done for you. Second, the fruit is often picked and prepared at peak freshness, making for especially bold flavor. And third, baby food usually contains a touch of vitamin C, which helps the fruit keep its vibrant color. A small 4-ounce jar is the perfect portion to use in these recipes (see the Honeyed Apricot and Banana marshmallows, page 39).

KEY LIME PIE MARSHMALLOWS

About 2 dozen 1 1/2-inch mallows

Lightly coat an 8-by-8-inch baking pan with cooking spray.

WHISK TOGETHER the gelatin, key lime juice, and cold water in a small bowl. Let it soften for 5 minutes.

STIR TOGETHER the sugar, 1/4 cup of the corn syrup, water, and salt in a medium saucepan over high heat. Boil, stirring occasionally, until the temperature reaches 240°F. Meanwhile, pour the remaining 1/4 cup corn syrup into the bowl of an electric mixer fitted with the whisk attachment. Microwave the gelatin on high until completely melted, about 30 seconds, and pour it into the corn syrup. Set the mixer to low and keep it running.

WHEN THE SYRUP reaches 240°F, slowly pour it into the mixer bowl. Increase the speed to medium and beat for 5 minutes. Increase the speed to medium-high and beat for 5 more minutes. Increase to the highest setting, add the vanilla and food coloring, and beat for 1 minute more. The finished marshmallow will be tripled in volume. Pour it into the prepared pan, using an offset spatula to smooth it into the corners. Sprinkle graham cracker crumbs evenly over top. Let it set for 6 hours in a cool, dry place.

Use a knife to loosen the marshmallow from the edges of the pan and invert the slab onto a work surface. Sprinkle with graham cracker crumbs. Cut it into pieces and dip the sticky edges in more crumbs, patting off the excess.

MORE MALLOWS

Lemonade Marshmallows: Swap out the lime juice in the Bloom stage for 6 tablespoons freshly squeezed lemon juice and decrease the cold water to 2 tablespoons. Beat in 2 teaspoons grated lemon zest during the last minute of beating and tint the marshmallow with a bit of yellow food coloring. For finishing, whisk 3 packets of True Lemon powder into 1/2 cup Classic Coating.

the bloom
- 4 1/2 teaspoons unflavored powdered gelatin
- 1/4 cup freshly squeezed key lime juice
- 1/4 cup cold water

the syrup
- 1 cup sugar
- 1/2 cup light corn syrup, divided
- 1/4 cup water
- 1/8 teaspoon salt

the mallowing
- 1 teaspoon pure vanilla extract
  Green gel food coloring
- 1 cup graham cracker crumbs* (about 8 store-bought cracker sheets, or see page 27 for Homemade Graham Cracker recipes)

* For a great textural element, pulse the crackers in a food processor to get nubbly, not-too-finely ground crumbs. Or forgo the crumbs altogether in favor of 1/2 cup Classic Coating (page 8), whisked with a few packets of True Lime powder (found by the drink mixes in supermarkets).

CREAMSICLE MARSHMALLOWS

About 2 dozen 1 ½-inch mallows

WHIP UP A BATCH of Classic Vanilla Marshmallow batter, reducing the vanilla extract to 1 teaspoon. Beat in the orange oil, just a couple drops at a time, stopping the mixer to taste the marshmallow after every addition. Beat in the food coloring, drop by drop, until you get a soft, dreamy orange. Beat 1 to 2 minutes more on the highest speed; the finished marshmallow will be tripled in volume. Pour it into the prepared pan, using an offset spatula to smooth it into the corners. Sift coating evenly and generously over top. Let set for about 6 hours in a cool, dry place.

Use a knife to loosen the marshmallow from the edges of the pan. Invert the slab onto a coating-dusted work surface and dust it with more coating. Cut it into pieces and dip the sticky edges in more coating, patting off the excess.

the mallowing
- 1 batch Classic Vanilla batter (page 16)
- 6 to 8 drops pure orange oil Orange gel food coloring
- ½ cup Classic Coating (page 8), plus more for dusting

PLAYING WITH ESSENTIAL OILS

Essential oils are a fabulous way to get intense, natural flavors into your mallows. Pure citrus varieties like lemon, lime, and orange (as in the little Creamsicle gems here) are an obvious choice, but options abound and are easily found in natural-food stores. When shopping for essential oils to use in cooking and confections, read the labels carefully to find ones that are 100% pure. Be sure to look for therapeutic-grade oils, which are safe for food use (perfume-grade oils are not).

Think exotic, earthy, floral, or herbal variations: basil oil in strawberry marshmallows, raspberry with rose oil, cinnamon oil straight up, peppermint with chocolate, lavender and vanilla, or a blend of oils to create a chai-inspired mallow. The blank canvas of a plain marshmallow is perfect for just about anything you want to throw at it.

However, be judicious when adding essential oils to marshmallow batter. One drop can go a long way, and one drop too many can mean the difference between a heavenly mallow and one that tastes vaguely like your grandmother's perfume collection. So add a drop or two to start, beat it in, stop the mixer, and taste before adding more. Keep in mind that some flavors will also bloom further as the marshmallow sits. With essential oils, less is almost always more.

PUMPKIN SPICE MARSHMALLOWS

About 2 dozen 1 1/2-inch mallows

Lightly coat an 8-by-8-inch baking pan with cooking spray.

🌸 **WHISK TOGETHER** the gelatin and cold water in a small heatproof bowl and let it soften for 5 minutes.

💧 **STIR TOGETHER** the sugar, 1/4 cup of the corn syrup, water, and salt in a medium saucepan. Bring the syrup to a boil over high heat, stirring occasionally, until it reaches 250°F. Meanwhile, pour the remaining 1/4 cup corn syrup into the bowl of an electric mixer fitted with the whisk attachment. Microwave the gelatin on high until completely melted, about 30 seconds. Pour it into the corn syrup. Set the mixer to low and keep it running.

⬡ **IN A SMALL BOWL,** whisk together the pumpkin puree with the cinnamon, ginger, nutmeg, and vanilla. When the syrup reaches 250°F, slowly pour it into the mixer bowl. Increase the speed to medium and beat for 5 minutes. Increase to medium-high and beat for 5 minutes more. Beat on the highest setting for another minute. Beat in the vanilla and pumpkin mixture on high speed for 1 final minute. The finished marshmallow will be tripled in volume. If you want to bump up the color, beat in a drop or two of orange food coloring.

Quickly give the marshmallow batter a fold to ensure the pumpkin is fully incorporated. Pour it into the prepared pan, using an offset spatula to smooth it into the corners. Generously sprinkle with the cinnamon coating. Let set for at least 6 hours.

Use a knife to loosen the marshmallow from the edges of the pan. Invert the slab onto a work surface sprinkled with coating and dust with more coating. Cut it into pieces and dip the sticky edges in more coating, patting off the excess.

🌸 **the bloom**
- 5 teaspoons unflavored powdered gelatin
- 1/2 cup cold water

💧 **the syrup**
- 3/4 cup sugar
- 1/2 cup light corn syrup, divided
- 1/4 cup water
- 1/4 teaspoon salt

⬡ **the mallowing**
- 1/3 cup canned pumpkin puree*
- 1/2 teaspoon ground cinnamon
- 1/4 teaspoon ground ginger
- 1/8 teaspoon freshly grated nutmeg
- 1 teaspoon pure vanilla extract
  Orange gel food coloring, optional
- 1/2 cup Classic Coating (page 8), whisked with 1/4 teaspoon ground cinnamon

* Be sure to buy 100% pure canned pumpkin puree, without added sugar or spices. I like Libby's brand for its thick texture and vibrant color and flavor.

HONEYED APRICOT MARSHMALLOWS

About 2 dozen 1 ½-inch mallows

Generously dust a baking sheet with Classic Coating (page 8).

WHISK THE GELATIN with the baby food and cold nectar in a small, heatproof bowl. Let it soften for 10 minutes.

WHISK TOGETHER the corn syrup and honey in a small bowl. Pour ¼ cup of the mixture (roughly half) into the bowl of an electric mixer and scrape the remainder into a medium saucepan. Add the sugar, apricot nectar, and salt and bring to a boil, stirring occasionally, until it reaches 250°F. Microwave the gelatin on high until completely melted, about 1 minute, and pour it into the mixer bowl. Set the mixer to low and keep it running.

WHEN THE SYRUP reaches 250°F, slowly pour it into the mixer bowl. Increase the speed to medium and beat for 5 minutes. Increase to medium-high and beat for 3 more minutes. Increase to the highest setting and beat for 3 to 4 minutes more, adding the vanilla and food coloring in the last minute. The finished marshmallow will be tripled in volume. Load it into a pastry bag fitted with a large round tip. With a circular motion, pipe the batter into little clouds. Dust with coating and let them set for 6 hours in a cool, dry place.

MORE MALLOWS

Banana Marshmallows: Decrease the gelatin to 5 teaspoons and add 2 tablespoons cold water in the Bloom stage. Replace the apricot baby food with banana, skip the nectar, and replace the honey with corn syrup. Cook the syrup to 242°F to 245°F. Beat the batter for 5 minutes on medium, 5 minutes on medium-high, and 7 minutes on the highest setting, beating in the vanilla and some yellow food coloring in the last minute. Make these a full day ahead—the banana flavor will be much perkier after a 24-hour rest.

the bloom
- 2 tablespoons unflavored powdered gelatin
- 1 4-ounce jar apricot baby food*
- ¼ cup cold apricot nectar

the syrup
- ¼ cup corn syrup
- ¼ cup honey
- ¾ cup sugar
- ⅓ cup apricot nectar
- ⅛ teaspoon fine sea salt

the mallowing
- 1 teaspoon pure vanilla extract
  Orange food coloring, optional
- ½ cup Classic Coating (page 8), plus more for dusting

* Baby food is a smart and time-saving ingredient in fruit-flavored marshmallows. It has bold, pure flavor without added sugar, and it contains vitamin C, which keeps fruit from oxidizing and muddying your mallows' color. Plus all the prep work has been done for you!

TRICKS FOR FANCY MARSHMALLOW SHAPES

Maybe you're thinking that cutting the cured mallow slab into cubes is all you can do. Not so! Experiment with different tools and techniques to twist and stretch your mallows into cute and creative homespun confections.

HOMEMADE LAYERED MALLOWS

As if from-scratch marshmallows weren't delightful enough, you can also easily layer different colors and flavors in the same pan. I mean, a rainbow marshmallow? Baskets of kittens might start raining from the sky from all the cuteness.

Make one (or a double) batch of Classic Vanilla Marshmallows, but reduce the whipping time by about a minute so the batter won't set too quickly. Have nearby as many different bowls as you want colors of mallows. Working swiftly, divide your batter among the bowls. Tint each batter with gel food coloring, stirring each energetically to blend the color as quickly as possible. Pour and spread the colors into the prepared pan one at a time, layering them on top of one another. Dust with coating and let set. (For more tips on manipulating mallow batter, see page 90.)

You can also layer different flavors in the same pan by making separate batches and layering them. Some of my favorite combinations are Neopolitan (layers of Chocolate, Vanilla, and Strawberry), Malibu Marshmallows layered with Key Lime Pie, and PB&J.

MALLOW LOLLIPOPS

To coil lollipops, start by lining a baking sheet with a silicone baking mat. Coat it with cooking spray and wipe off excess. Whip up a batch of marshmallow batter and load it into a pastry bag fitted with a medium round tip. Pipe long lines in parallel rows across the baking sheet. Do not dust with coating. Let set for about 1 hour, or until the marshmallow can be gently lifted without breaking. Roll the lines of mallow into coils and lay them flat on a coating-dusted baking sheet. Dust with more coating and let them cure for at least 3 hours before inserting lollipop sticks, pushing them almost all the way through the top so the coil holds together. Brush off excess coating with a pastry brush.

TWISTED MARSHMALLOW ROPES

To make the tricolored ropes shown on the cover, follow the technique of piping long lines of mallow batter onto a prepared baking sheet, as described in Mallow Lollipops. After the marshmallow has set for about 30 minutes but is still tacky, lay two ropes snugly side by side. Stack a third rope in the groove where the first two meet. Hold one end of the rope in each hand and twist them tightly together. (This fun job is even easier if a friend helps!) Set the twisted rope on the baking sheet and dust with Classic Coating. Let set for at least 4 hours, then trim the ends.

HAPPY HOUR
Cocktail-Inspired Marshmallows

A great man once said, candy is dandy, but liquor is quicker. Have truer words ever been spoken? Marshmallows are the ultimate happy candy, but add a few shots of your favorite booze and—BAM!—instant confection celebration for the adult set. Overconsumption of any of the following marshmallows may result in loud laughter, a lackadaisical attitude toward clothing, and/or suddenly thinking you are really great at karaoke.

MARGARITA MARSHMALLOWS

About 2 dozen 1 ½-inch mallows

Lightly coat an 8-by-8-inch baking pan with cooking spray.

WHISK THE GELATIN with the lime juice, tequila, and water in a small bowl. Let it soften for 10 minutes.

STIR TOGETHER the sugar, ¼ cup of the corn syrup, tequila, and salt in a medium saucepan over high heat. Boil, stirring occasionally, until it reaches 242°F to 245°F. Meanwhile, pour the remaining ¼ cup corn syrup into the bowl of an electric mixer fitted with the whisk attachment. Microwave the gelatin on high until completely melted, about 30 seconds, and pour it into the corn syrup. Set the mixer to low and keep it running.

WHEN THE SYRUP reaches 242°F to 245°F, slowly pour it into the mixer bowl. Increase the speed to medium and beat for 5 minutes. Increase to medium-high and beat 5 minutes more. Increase to the highest setting and beat for 1 to 2 more minutes. The finished marshmallow will be more than doubled in volume. Add a bit of yellow-green food coloring, if you wish. Pour the marshmallow into the prepared pan, using an offset spatula to smooth it into the corners. Sift coating evenly over top. Let it set for at least 8 hours in a cool, dry place.

Use a knife to loosen the marshmallow from the edges of the pan. Invert the slab onto a coating-dusted work surface and dust it with more coating. Cut it into pieces. Roll the sticky sides of the mallows in pearl sugar.

Boozy mallows won't reach the same level of fluff as their virgin counterparts—the alcohol tends to weigh things down (insert peanut gallery comment here). They're ideal for piping into molds for a fun addition to a party table or, if you want them to appear puffier, just use a smaller pan.

the bloom
- 5 teaspoons unflavored powdered gelatin
- ¼ cup freshly squeezed lime juice
- 2 tablespoons tequila (80 proof)
- ¼ cup cold water

the syrup
- ¾ cup sugar
- ½ cup light corn syrup, divided
- 2 tablespoons tequila
- ¼ teaspoon salt

the mallowing
- Yellow-green gel food coloring, optional
- ½ cup Classic Coating (page 8), plus more for dusting*
- ¼ cup Swedish pearl sugar, for rolling**

* To add an extra hit of lime, whisk in a few packets of True Lime powder, available by the drink mixes in supermarkets.

** Swedish pearl sugar gives these mallows a "salted rim" kind of vibe, but with a sweet crunch. You can find it at specialty stores and online.

BUTTERED RUM MARSHMALLOWS

About 2 dozen 1 1/2-inch mallows

Lightly coat an 8-by-8-inch baking pan with cooking spray.

WHISK TOGETHER the gelatin, cold water, and rum in a small bowl. Let it soften for 10 minutes.

STIR TOGETHER the sugars, 1/4 cup of the corn syrup, water, rum, and salt in a large saucepan over high heat. Boil, stirring occasionally, until it reaches 242°F to 245°F. Be prepared to monitor the heat; the syrup will bubble up suddenly around 190°F as the alcohol starts to boil. Meanwhile, pour the remaining 1/4 cup corn syrup into the bowl of an electric mixer fitted with the whisk attachment. Place the softened butter in a medium bowl. Microwave the gelatin on high until completely melted, about 30 seconds, and pour it into the corn syrup. Set the mixer to low and keep it running.

WHEN THE SYRUP reaches 242°F to 245°F, slowly pour it into the mixer bowl. Increase the speed to medium and beat for 5 minutes. Beat for 5 minutes more at medium-high speed. Beat on the highest speed for 1 to 2 more minutes, adding the vanilla. The finished marshmallow will be doubled in volume. Quickly scoop about a quarter of the batter into the bowl with the softened butter and whisk to blend. Scrape the buttered batter into the rest of the batter and fold to blend well. Pour the marshmallow into the prepared pan. Sift coating evenly over top. Let set for 8 hours in a cool, dry place.

Use a knife to loosen the marshmallow from the edges of the pan. Invert the slab onto a coating-dusted work surface. Cut into pieces, dusting the sticky edges with more coating.

These addictive confections have deep notes of brown sugar, a rich butter flavor, and just a hint of booziness. Perfect for adult s'mores, or, freshly prepared and unset, this mallow batter makes for a dangerously delicious ice-cream topping.

the bloom

- 4 1/2 teaspoons unflavored powdered gelatin
- 1/3 cup cold water
- 1 tablespoon dark rum (80 proof)*

the syrup

- 1/2 cup lightly packed dark brown sugar
- 1/2 cup granulated sugar
- 1/2 cup light corn syrup, divided
- 1/4 cup water
- 3 tablespoons dark rum
- 1/2 teaspoon salt

the mallowing

- 1 teaspoon pure vanilla extract
- 2 tablespoons unsalted butter, soft and well-stirred
- 1/2 cup Classic Coating (page 8), plus more for dusting

* For baking and candymaking, I love Myers's dark rum for its rich, bold flavor. A 2-ounce bottle is the perfect amount.

FUZZY NAVEL MARSHMALLOWS

About 2 dozen 1 ½-inch mallows

Lightly coat an 8-by-8-inch baking pan with cooking spray.

WHISK TOGETHER the gelatin, orange juice, and schnapps. Let it soften for 10 minutes.

PLACE THE SUGAR, ¼ cup of the corn syrup, water, schnapps, and salt in a medium saucepan over medium-high heat. Boil, stirring occasionally, until it hits 240°F. Meanwhile, pour the remaining ¼ cup corn syrup into the bowl of an electric mixer fitted with the whisk attachment. Microwave the gelatin on high until completely melted, about 30 seconds, and pour it into the mixer bowl. Turn the mixer on low and keep it running.

WHEN THE SYRUP reaches 240°F, slowly pour it into the mixer bowl. Increase the speed to medium and beat for 5 minutes. Increase to medium-high and beat 5 more minutes. Increase to the highest setting and beat for 2 to 3 minutes more. The finished marshmallow will be more than double in volume. Pour it into the prepared pan, using an offset spatula to smooth it into the corners. Sift coating evenly over top. Let it set for 8 hours in a cool, dry place.

Use a knife to loosen the marshmallow from the edges of the pan. Invert the slab onto a coating-dusted work surface and dust it with more coating. Cut it into pieces and dip the sticky edges in more coating, patting off the excess.

the bloom
4 ½ teaspoons unflavored powdered gelatin
½ cup cold, freshly squeezed orange juice
2 tablespoons peach schnapps (30 proof)

the syrup
¾ cup sugar
½ cup light corn syrup, divided
¼ cup water
2 tablespoons peach schnapps
⅛ teaspoon salt

the mallowing
½ cup Classic Coating (page 8), plus more for dusting

TIPS FOR MALLOWING WITH BOOZE

Making a boozy marshmallow is tricky business. The chemistry hedges on the liquor's proof, the number that indicates its percentage of alcohol; that number is double the percentage (40 proof means 20% alcohol). If you want to experiment, your best bet is to look for a recipe that calls for a liquor that has a similar proof as the one you want to try. For example, to make Chambord marshmallows, follow the Crème de Menthe recipe—both liqueurs are about 30 proof.

CRÈME DE MENTHE MARSHMALLOWS

About 2 dozen 1 ½-inch mallows

Lightly coat an 8-by-8-inch baking pan with cooking spray.

🌀 **WHISK TOGETHER** the gelatin, cold water, and crème de menthe in a small bowl. Let it soften for 10 minutes.

💧 **STIR TOGETHER** the sugar, ¼ cup of the corn syrup, crème de menthe, water, and salt in a medium saucepan over high heat. Boil, stirring occasionally, until the temperature reaches 240°F. Pour the remaining ¼ cup corn syrup into the bowl of an electric mixer fitted with the whisk attachment. Microwave the gelatin on high until completely melted, about 30 seconds, and pour it into the mixer bowl. Set the mixer to low and keep it running.

🌸 **WHEN THE SYRUP** reaches 240°F, slowly pour it into the mixer bowl. Increase the speed to medium and beat for 5 minutes. Increase to medium-high and beat for 3 more minutes. Beat on the highest setting for 1 to 2 minutes more, adding the vanilla. The finished marshmallow will be more than doubled in volume. Use a spatula to quickly fold in the chocolate chips; too much stirring can cause the bits to melt and give the candy a muddy look. Pour the marshmallow into the prepared pan. Sift coating evenly over top. Let set for at least 6 hours in a cool, dry place.

Use a knife to loosen the marshmallow from the edges of the pan. Invert the slab onto a coating-dusted work surface. Cut it into pieces and dust the sticky edges with more coating. Line a baking sheet with parchment paper or a silicone baking mat. Dip the bottom half of each mallow in the melted chocolate and place on the baking sheet. Refrigerate until chocolate is firm, about 10 minutes.

Crème de menthe is an intensely minty, bright green liqueur; it adds incredible flavor and color to these mallows. If you're a teetotaler or under age 21, omit the liqueur from the bloom and the syrup, and beat in about ½ teaspoon peppermint extract and some green food coloring along with the vanilla.

🌀 **the bloom**
- 4 teaspoons unflavored powdered gelatin
- ⅓ cup cold water
- 2 tablespoons crème de menthe (30 proof)

💧 **the syrup**
- 1 cup sugar
- ½ cup light corn syrup, divided
- ¼ cup crème de menthe
- ¼ cup water
- ¼ teaspoon salt

🌸 **the mallowing**
- 1 teaspoon pure vanilla extract
- ½ cup mini semisweet chocolate chips*
- ½ cup Classic Coating (page 8), plus more for dusting
- 8 ounces bittersweet chocolate chips (60% to 70% cacao), melted and slightly cooled

* *Minis are recommended instead of regular chips or chopped chocolate because they distribute so nicely throughout the candy, make for cleanly cut marshmallows, and resist melting.*

MALIBU MARSHMALLOWS

About 2 dozen 1 ½-inch mallows

Lightly coat an 8-by-8-inch baking pan with cooking spray. Spread about ½ cup toasted coconut evenly in the bottom of the pan.

WHISK THE GELATIN together with the coconut water and coconut rum in a small bowl. Let it soften for 10 minutes.

STIR TOGETHER the sugar, ¼ cup of the corn syrup, coconut water, coconut rum, and salt in a medium saucepan over high heat. Boil, stirring occasionally, until it hits 240°F. Meanwhile, pour the remaining ¼ cup corn syrup into the bowl of an electric mixer fitted with the whisk attachment. Microwave the gelatin on high until completely melted, about 30 seconds, and pour it into the mixer bowl. Set the mixer to low and keep it running.

WHEN THE SYRUP reaches 240°F, slowly pour it into the mixer bowl in a steady stream. Increase the speed to medium and beat for 5 minutes. Beat for 3 minutes more at medium-high speed. Beat on the highest speed for 1 to 2 minutes more, adding the vanilla. The finished marshmallow will be more than doubled in volume. Pour it into the prepared pan, using an offset spatula to smooth it into the corners. Sprinkle toasted coconut generously over top. Let set for about 6 hours in a cool, dry place.

Use a knife to loosen the marshmallow from the edges of the pan. Invert the slab onto a work surface. Cut it into pieces and dip the sticky edges in more toasted coconut.

If booze isn't your thing, you can make an equally delicious coconut marshmallow without it. Add about ½ teaspoon coconut extract to the Classic Vanilla Marshmallow recipe (page 16), rolling the mallows in toasted coconut.

the bloom
- 5 teaspoons unflavored powdered gelatin
- ½ cup cold coconut water*
- 2 tablespoons coconut rum, such as Malibu (40 proof)

the syrup
- ¾ cup sugar
- ½ cup light corn syrup, divided
- ¼ cup coconut water
- 2 tablespoons coconut rum
- ¼ teaspoon salt

the mallowing
- 1 teaspoon pure vanilla extract
- 1 cup shredded, sweetened coconut, toasted*

* Coconut water can be found in natural-food stores and large supermarkets. If unavailable, use regular water.

* Toast coconut by spreading it in an even layer on a small baking sheet and baking at 350°F for about 10 minutes, stirring often to prevent burning.

FOR THE MALLOW CONNOISSEUR

Gourmet Flavors and Textures

Do you scour farmers markets and specialty grocers looking for the odd and unusual? Are you the one in your group of friends who suggests the new Vietnamese place when everyone else wants to go for burgers and beer? Do the previous recipes for vanilla and fruit marshmallows have you scoffing at my safe zone? Well, discerning food people, here are a few recipes fit for the daring connoisseur.

MAPLE-BACON MARSHMALLOWS

About 2 dozen 1 ½-inch mallows

Lightly coat an 8-by-8-inch baking pan with cooking spray.

WHISK TOGETHER the gelatin and cold water in a small bowl. Let it soften for 5 minutes.

STIR TOGETHER the sugar, maple syrup, corn syrup, water, and salt in a medium saucepan. Bring it to a boil over high heat, stirring occasionally, until it hits 240°F. Be prepared to lower the heat as needed—this syrup likes to bubble up. Microwave the gelatin on high until completely melted, about 30 seconds. Pour it into the bowl of a stand mixer fitted with the whisk attachment. Set the mixer to low and keep it running.

WHEN THE SYRUP reaches 240°F, slowly pour it into the mixer bowl. Increase the speed to medium and beat for 5 minutes. Increase to medium-high and beat for 3 more minutes. Add the cinnamon, increase to the highest speed, and beat for 1 minute more. Quickly fold in the bacon bits. Pour the marshmallow into the prepared pan. Sift coating over top. Let it set for 6 hours in a cool, dry place. Use a knife to loosen the marshmallow from the edges of the pan. Invert the slab onto a work surface. Cut it into pieces and dust them with more coating.

MORE MALLOWS

The Elvis: Honor the King. Whip up a batch of Banana Marshmallow (page 39). Transfer about a quarter of the batter to a small bowl with 3 tablespoons peanut butter, whisking to blend well. Swirl the peanut butter marshmallow into the rest of the banana mallow batter as you fold in the amount of crispy candied bacon bits from the Maple-Bacon Marshmallow recipe. *Thank you. Thank you very much.*

the bloom
4 ½ teaspoons unflavored powdered gelatin
½ cup cold water

the syrup
⅔ cup sugar
½ cup Grade A dark or Grade B maple syrup*
¼ cup light corn syrup
¼ cup water
¼ teaspoon salt

the mallowing
⅛ teaspoon ground cinnamon
½ cup (about 1 ½ ounces) finely chopped candied bacon*
½ cup Classic Coating (page 8), plus more for dusting

* The key to getting real maple flavor is using a dark amber Grade A or Grade B syrup, which are bolder than lighter Grade A varieties.

* To make candied bacon, lay 6 or 7 bacon slices on a wire rack set over a sheet pan lined with foil. Combine ¼ cup light brown sugar with ⅛ teaspoon ground cinnamon. Rub over both sides of bacon. Bake at 350°F until deeply caramelized, 30 to 35 minutes. Let cool before chopping into bits.

PINEAPPLE-ROSEMARY MARSHMALLOWS

About 2 dozen 1 ½-inch mallows

Lightly coat an 8-by-8-inch baking pan with cooking spray.

Keep a ½-cup measuring cup nearby to gauge the reducing juice for the bloom.

PLACE THE JUICE and rosemary leaves in a large saucepan over high heat; boil until reduced by half, about 10 minutes. Transfer the juice (with the leaves; it's OK if they've discolored) to a small heatproof bowl and place it in the freezer to cool down. When it's cold to the touch, pour it through a sieve into a small heatproof bowl, discarding the leaves. Whisk the cold water into the juice, followed by the gelatin. Let it soften for 5 minutes.

STIR TOGETHER the sugar, ¼ cup of the corn syrup, juice, water, and salt in a medium saucepan. Bring to a boil over high heat, stirring occasionally, until it reaches 240°F. Meanwhile, pour the remaining ¼ cup corn syrup into the bowl of an electric mixer fitted with the whisk attachment. Microwave the gelatin on high until completely melted, about 30 seconds, and pour it into the mixer bowl. Set the mixer to low and keep it running.

WHEN THE SYRUP reaches 240°F, slowly pour it into the mixer bowl in a steady stream. Increase the speed to medium and beat for 5 minutes. Increase to medium-high and beat for 5 more minutes. Beat on the highest setting for 1 minute more, adding the vanilla and food coloring in the last minute. The finished marshmallow will be tripled in volume. Pour it into the prepared pan and sift coating over top. Let it set for 8 hours in a cool, dry place.

Use a knife to loosen the marshmallow from the edges of the pan. Invert the slab onto a coating-dusted work surface. Cut it into pieces and dip the sticky edges in more coating, patting off the excess.

the bloom

- 1 cup unsweetened pineapple juice
- 2 teaspoons fresh rosemary leaves
- ¼ cup cold water
- 4 ½ teaspoons unflavored powdered gelatin

the syrup

- ¾ cup sugar
- ½ cup light corn syrup, divided
- ¼ cup unsweetened pineapple juice
- ¼ cup water
- ¼ teaspoon salt

the mallowing

- 1 teaspoon pure vanilla extract
  Yellow gel food coloring
- ½ cup Classic Coating (page 8), plus more for dusting

Pineapple is one of those crazy fruits that doesn't play well with gelatin; it contains an enzyme that will keep the proteins in gelatin from setting. So we whip that unruly enzyme into submission by boiling the juice first, to ensure that we've weakened its defiant nature. The bonus is that the reduced juice packs a ton of flavor, and heating it gives us a chance to steep fresh rosemary right into the bloom.

MORE MALLOWS

Spiced-Cherry Marshmallows: Swap out the pineapple juice in the Bloom and Syrup stages for unsweetened tart cherry juice. Place 1 cinnamon stick, 1 star anise, and 2 cloves into the reducing juice. Cover the pan and let the juice steep for 15 minutes before cooling it in the freezer. Use a few drops of red food coloring to bump up the pink color of the mallows. Whisk 1 teaspoon ground cinnamon into the Classic Coating.

STEEPING IN FLAVORS

This recipe is only the beginning when it comes to steeping bold and interesting flavors into mallows. In fact, you can take just about any recipe from the "Fresh and Fruity" chapter and steep in beautiful herbal and floral pairings just by first heating the fruit juice or puree. Some of my favorite combinations are strawberry-basil, lemon thyme, and raspberry-rose. The key is to find organic or unsprayed herbs and flowers before adding them into the mix.

Another great way to steep elegant flavors is by using teas. Rather than plain water in your bloom and syrup, substitute a super-strong batch of tea. Smoky earl grey, rose hip, mint, and chai blends are delicious. Use a dab of food coloring to give a soft hue to the mallows, just enough to suggest their flavor.

SEA SALT CARAMEL SWIRL MARSHMALLOWS

About 2 dozen 1 1/2-inch mallows

Lightly coat an 8-by-8-inch baking pan with cooking spray and wipe away any excess.

STIR TOGETHER the sugar, water, and corn syrup in a small saucepan over high heat. Stir until the sugar is dissolved and the syrup comes to a bubble. From this point on, don't stir the syrup; just occasionally swirl the pan gently. When the caramel reaches a light amber color, remove the pan from the heat and quickly whisk in the cream. The caramel will bubble violently, so be careful. Whisk in the salt. Transfer the caramel to a medium bowl.

WHIP UP A BATCH of Classic Vanilla batter. Working quickly, scoop about a quarter of the finished batter into the bowl with the caramel. Whisk the mixture together until well blended. Scrape the caramel marshmallow back into the bowl with the vanilla batter and, using a large spatula and a figure-eight motion, fold and swirl the two together. Pour the marshmallow into the prepared pan, using an offset spatula to smooth it into the corners and flatten the top. Sift coating evenly and generously over the top. Let it set for 8 hours in a cool, dry place.

Use a knife to loosen the marshmallow from the edges of the pan. Invert the slab onto a coating-dusted work surface and dust it with more coating. Cut it into pieces and dip the sticky edges in more coating, patting off the excess. After a day or two of storage, these mallows may need to be redusted with coating.

If you're crunched for time or if caramel-making terrifies you, a half cup of a high-quality store-bought caramel sauce (seasoned with an extra hit of salt) makes for a decent stand-in.

the swirl
- 1/3 cup sugar
- 2 tablespoons water
- 1 teaspoon light corn syrup
- 3 tablespoons heavy cream
- 1/8 teaspoon sea salt

the mallowing
- 1 batch Classic Vanilla batter (page 16)*
- 1/2 cup Classic Coating (page 8), plus more for dusting

* Increase the salt to 1/4 teaspoon in the syrup.

SALTED PEANUT MARSHMALLOWS

About 2 dozen 1 ½-inch mallows

WHIP UP A BATCH of Classic Vanilla batter. After beating in the vanilla, fold in the coarsely chopped peanuts. Pour the marshmallow into the prepared pan. Completely cover the surface with a generous amount of finely chopped peanuts, reserving the remainder. Let it set for 6 hours in a cool, dry place.

Use a knife to loosen the marshmallow from the edges of the pan. Invert the slab onto a work surface. Cover with a generous coating of finely chopped peanuts. Cut the slab into pieces and dip the sticky edges in more finely chopped peanuts.

SWEET AND SALTY

Nothing makes a sweet treat more crave-worthy than a good hit of salt, and it's an especially crafty way to temper the sweetness of marshmallows. Try rolling Deeply Chocolate Marshmallows (page 18) in crushed potato chips. Or mix marshmallow batter with a whole bunch of popcorn and other little sweet and salty nubs to make the world's best popcorn balls (see Ballpark Popcorn Balls, page 91).

the mallowing

- 1 batch Classic Vanilla batter (page 16)
- 2/3 cup roasted salted peanuts,* coarsely chopped
- 1 ¼ cup roasted salted peanuts, finely chopped

* When shopping for salted peanuts, be sure to check the ingredients list. Some varieties sneak in additional flavors like garlic and paprika—great with a few beers, but not so tasty for mallowing. Look for one that contains simply peanuts, oil, and salt; the "cocktail" variety is usually a good bet.

MALLOWS IN THE RAW

About 2 dozen 1 ½-inch mallows

Lightly coat an 8-by-8-inch baking pan with cooking spray.

WHISK TOGETHER the gelatin and cold water in a small bowl. Let it soften for 5 minutes.

STIR TOGETHER the turbinado sugar, agave syrup, water, and salt in a large saucepan over high heat. Boil, stirring occasionally, until the temperature hits 248°F to 250°F. Microwave the gelatin on high until completely melted, about 30 seconds, and pour it into the bowl of a stand mixer fitted with the whisk attachment. Set the speed to low and keep it running.

WHEN THE SYRUP reaches 248°F to 250°F, slowly pour it into the mixer bowl in a steady stream. Increase the speed to medium and beat for 5 minutes. Increase to medium-high and beat for 5 more minutes. Add vanilla and beat on the highest setting for 1 minute more. The finished marshmallow will be tripled in volume. Pour it into the prepared pan, using an offset spatula to smooth it into the corners. Sift coating generously over top. Let set for 8 hours in a cool, dry place.

Use a knife to loosen the marshmallow from the edges of the pan. Invert the slab onto a coating-dusted work surface and dust it with more coating. Cut it into pieces and dip the sticky edges in more coating, patting off the excess.

Maybe your child has allergies to refined sugar. Maybe you just want a more natural approach to the common s'more. Or maybe, like me, you dig playing mad scientist with sweeteners. Whatever the reason, you won't miss the so-bad-it's-good stuff with these unrefined mallows, which you can flavor by adding extracts and candy oils. Or use this alternative sweetening technique for recipes in this book that call for granulated white sugar and corn syrup.

the bloom
- 5 teaspoons unflavored powdered gelatin
- ½ cup cold water

the syrup
- ¾ cup turbinado sugar*
- ½ cup light agave syrup
- ½ cup water
- ¼ teaspoon salt

the mallowing
- 1 teaspoon pure vanilla extract
- ½ cup Classic Coating (page 8), plus more for dusting*

* This coarse, tan sugar is sold under the brand name Sugar in the Raw. You can buy it in bulk at natural-food stores.

* To be truly in the raw, use plain cornstarch or potato starch.

MANGO-CHILE-LIME MARSHMALLOWS

About 2 dozen 1 ½-inch mallows

Lightly coat an 8-by-8-inch baking pan with cooking spray.

🌸 **WHISK TOGETHER** the gelatin, mango puree, lime juice, and cold water in a small heatproof bowl. Let it soften for 10 minutes.

💧 **STIR TOGETHER** the sugar, ¼ cup of the corn syrup, mango puree, water, cayenne pepper, and salt in a medium saucepan over high heat. Boil until it hits 242°F to 245°F.

Use a rigid heatproof spatula to occasionally stir the syrup, scraping the bottom of the pan to keep the syrup from clinging and burning. This syrup also has a tendency to boil up high in the pan, so be prepared to adjust the heat to prevent it from bubbling over.

Pour the remaining ¼ cup corn syrup into the bowl of an electric mixer fitted with the whisk attachment. Microwave the gelatin on high until completely melted, about 30 seconds, and pour it into the corn syrup. Set the mixer speed to low and keep it running.

⚪ **WHEN THE SYRUP** reaches 242°F to 245°F, slowly pour it into the mixer bowl in a steady stream. If any syrup has burned on the bottom of the pan, don't fret—just don't scrape any burned bits into the batter. Increase the speed to medium and beat for 5 minutes. Increase to medium-high and beat for 5 more minutes. Beat on the highest setting for 1 to 2 minutes more, or until tripled in volume. Pour the marshmallow into the prepared pan and sift the coating over top. Let it set for 8 hours.

Use a knife to loosen the marshmallow from the pan, invert the slab onto a coating-covered work surface, and dust it with more coating. Cut it into pieces and dip the sticky edges in more coating, patting off the excess. These marshmallows may need to be redusted with coating after a day or two of storage.

To work the spicy-sweet angle in a whole different way, whip up some Aztec Chocolate marshmallows: Add the same amount of cayenne pepper listed in this recipe to Deeply Chocolate marshmallow batter (page 18).

🌸 **the bloom**
- 5 teaspoons unflavored powdered gelatin
- ½ cup mango puree
- 2 tablespoons freshly squeezed lime juice
- 2 tablespoons cold water

💧 **the syrup**
- ¾ cup sugar
- ½ cup light corn syrup, divided
- 2 tablespoons mango puree
- ¼ cup water
- ⅛ teaspoon cayenne pepper
- ¼ teaspoon salt

⚪ **the mallowing**
- ½ cup Classic Coating (page 8), plus more for dusting

FLUFFY PUFFS FOR GIFTING

Despite their sweetness and tender,
delicate chew, homemade marshmallows are sturdy
little buggers that resist smooshing and melting (except
when exposed to direct heat). Their mallowy moxie makes them
perfect for care packages and presents. You can pop them in a tin or
bag, but marshmallows are so awe inspiring and visually exciting all on their
own, they don't need much more than a plain cellophane bag tied with pretty
ribbon to make them gift-worthy. Here are a few of my favorite ideas for pulling
together perfect little holiday, housewarming, and hostess gifts.

HOT COCOA JARS: Fill a large Mason jar with all the dry ingredients for a soul-soothing batch of hot chocolate (see "Desserts Made Drinkable," page 94, for inspiration). Fit a square of vintage fabric over the lid and secure it with ribbon, tying on a handwritten recipe card listing the rest of the ingredients and cooking instructions. Pack it into a cute box or basket along with a big bag of homemade marshmallows. A fun mug makes the treat complete.

MARSHMALLOW CANDY BOX: Create your own confectionery masterpiece with an oversize box of "chocolates." Find a sturdy, shirt-sized gift box and line it with pretty patterned paper. Cut a few different flavors of marshmallow slabs into large squares or other shapes (and dip some in chocolate while you're at it!). Set each mallow into a cupcake liner and nestle them into the box, just like a classic bonbon sampler.

S'MORES KIT: Line a small rustic basket with a cheery printed napkin. Pack it with a bag of homemade mallows, graham crackers, and a few high-quality chocolate bars. Tie a bundle of wooden skewers with a sweet ribbon and call yourself a homespun gift goddess.

KIDS IN A CANDY STORE

Fun Flavors for Kids of All Ages

Since we're already all sugared up, I say we go all the way—which is to say, whip up a bunch of fluff in flavors that six-year-olds will lose their minds over. Get ready to play mad scientist with some true novelty flavors. I'm talking cake mix, rainbow sprinkles, Kool-Aid, and a dizzying array of whimsical ingredients. These recipes are the stuff kid-in-a-candy-store dreams are made of.

KOOL-AID MARSHMALLOWS

About 2 dozen 1 1/2-inch mallows

Lightly coat an 8-by-8-inch baking pan with cooking spray.

🌸 **WHISK TOGETHER** the Kool-Aid mix, cold water, and gelatin in a small bowl. Let it soften for 5 minutes.

💧 **STIR TOGETHER** the sugar, 1/4 cup of the corn syrup, water, and salt in a medium saucepan. Bring the syrup to a boil over high heat, stirring occasionally, until it reaches 240°F. Pour the remaining 1/4 cup corn syrup into the bowl of an electric mixer fitted with the whisk attachment. Microwave the gelatin on high until completely melted, about 30 seconds, and pour it into the mixer bowl. Set the mixer to low and keep it running.

⬡ **WHEN THE SYRUP** reaches 240°F, slowly pour it into the mixer bowl. Increase the speed to medium and beat for 5 minutes. Increase to medium-high and beat for 5 more minutes. Beat on the highest setting for 1 to 2 minutes more. The finished marshmallow will be tripled in volume. Pour it into the prepared pan, using an offset spatula to smooth it into the corners. Sift coating generously over top. Let it set for 6 hours in a cool, dry place.

Use a knife to loosen the marshmallow from the edges of the pan. Invert the slab onto a coating-dusted work surface and dust it with more coating. Cut into shapes and dip the sticky edges in Pop Rocks or more coating, patting off the excess.

As close to snack time as possible, roll the mallows in Pop Rocks so that they'll be cracking when you serve them!

🌸 **the bloom**
- 1 (.16-ounce) packet unsweetened Kool-Aid drink mix, any flavor*
- 1/2 cup cold water
- 5 teaspoons unflavored powdered gelatin

💧 **the syrup**
- 3/4 cup sugar
- 1/2 cup light corn syrup, divided
- 1/4 cup water
- 1/8 teaspoon salt

⬡ **the mallowing**
- 1/2 cup Classic Coating (page 8), plus more for dusting
- 4 packets Pop Rocks, for sprinkling (optional)

* I use Tropical Punch for these hot pink marshmallows.

FLUFFERNUTTER MARSHMALLOWS

About 2 dozen 1 ½-inch mallows

Lightly coat an 8-by-8-inch baking pan with cooking spray.

WHIP UP A BATCH of Classic Vanilla batter. Place the peanut butter in a medium bowl. Working quickly, scoop about a quarter of the batter into a bowl with the peanut butter. Stir until well blended. Scrape this peanut butter marshmallow back into the bowl with the vanilla batter, and, using a large spatula and a figure-eight motion, fold and swirl the two batters together. Pour it into the prepared pan, using an offset spatula to smooth it into the corners. Sift coating evenly over top. Let set for 6 hours in a cool, dry place.

Use a knife to loosen the marshmallow from the edges of the pan. Invert the slab onto a coating-dusted work surface and dust it with more coating. Cut into pieces and dip the sticky edges in more coating, patting off the excess.

MORE MALLOWS

PB&J Marshmallows: Layer 1 batch of Fluffernutter with 1 batch of Concord Grape Marshmallows (page 30). For tips on layering mallows, see the sidebar on page 41.

the mallowing

1 batch Classic Vanilla batter (page 16)

3 tablespoons creamy peanut butter*

½ cup Classic Coating (page 8), plus more for dusting

* For the best consistency, go with a commercial peanut butter, like Skippy. We're making marshmallow here, people. Not really the appropriate time for the natural stuff.

ROOT BEER FLOAT MARSHMALLOWS

About 2 dozen 1 ½-inch mallows

Lightly coat an 8-by-8-inch baking pan with cooking spray.

WHISK TOGETHER the gelatin and cold root beer in a small bowl. Let it soften for 5 minutes.

STIR TOGETHER the root beer, sugar, corn syrup, and salt in a medium saucepan over high heat. Boil until it hits 240°F. Microwave the gelatin on high until completely melted, about 30 seconds, and pour into the bowl of an electric mixer fitted with the whisk attachment. Set the mixer to low and keep it running.

WHEN THE SYRUP reaches 240°F, slowly pour it into the mixer bowl. Increase the speed to medium and beat for 5 minutes. Increase to medium-high and beat for 5 more minutes. Add vanilla and flavoring extract or oil (if using) and beat for 1 minute more. The finished marshmallow will be tripled in volume. Pour it into the prepared pan, using an offset spatula to smooth it into the corners. Sift coating generously over top. Let it set for 6 hours in a cool, dry place.

Use a knife to loosen the marshmallow from the edges of the pan. Invert the slab onto a coating-dusted work surface and dust it with more coating. Cut into pieces and dip the sticky edges in more coating, patting off the excess.

If there's a lot of fizz when you pour the root beer into the measuring cup, make sure it subsides completely to ensure you have the right amount.

MORE MALLOWS

Ginger Ale Marshmallows: Substitute a great-quality ginger ale for the root beer. To punch up the fiery ginger flavor even more, whisk ¼ teaspoon ground ginger into the Classic Coating.

the bloom

- 5 ½ teaspoons unflavored powdered gelatin
- ⅔ cup cold root beer*

the syrup

- ½ cup root beer
- ¾ cup sugar
- ¼ cup light corn syrup
- ¼ teaspoon salt

the mallowing

- 1 teaspoon pure vanilla extract
- Root beer extract or candy oil, optional
- ½ cup Classic Coating (page 8), plus more for dusting

* The brand of root beer will make a world of difference. A higher quality, specialty one (like Boylan's) will blossom as the marshmallow cures. If you can't get your hands on fancy root beer, try bumping up the flavor with a root beer candy oil or extract.

BUBBLE GUM MARSHMALLOWS

About 2 dozen 1 ½-inch mallows

Lightly coat an 8-by-8-inch baking pan with cooking spray.

WHIP UP A BATCH of Classic Vanilla batter, reducing the vanilla to 1 teaspoon. Add a few drops of pink food coloring and 3 or 4 drops of bubble gum flavoring and beat at high speed for a few seconds. Stop the mixer and taste the marshmallow before repeating the mixing process with just a drop or two more at a time. The finished marshmallow will be tripled in volume. Pour it into the prepared pan, using an offset spatula to smooth it into the corners. Sift coating evenly over top. Let it set for 6 hours in a cool, dry place.

Use a knife to loosen the marshmallow from the edges of the pan. Invert the slab onto a coating-dusted work surface and dust it with more coating. Cut into shapes and dip the sticky edges in more coating, patting off the excess.

the mallowing

1 batch Classic Vanilla batter (page 16)

Pink gel food coloring

Bubble gum candy oil

½ cup Classic Coating (page 8), plus more for dusting

THE SWEET WORLD OF CANDY OILS

Candy oils (my favorites are by LorAnn) are highly potent flavorings available online and at baking supply stores. A few drops go a long way, so add just one or two at a time, beat it into the batter, and then taste before adding more.

The array of available candy oils will blow your mind. This recipe calls for bubble gum, but novelty flavorings like cotton candy, Bavarian crème, and tutti-frutti are perfection in mallows. Now that you've got the basics of marshmallow-making down, let your imagination run wild with flavor and color combinations.

BIRTHDAY CAKE MARSHMALLOWS

About 2 dozen 1 1/2-inch mallows

Lightly coat an 8-by-8-inch baking pan with cooking spray.

WHIP UP A BATCH of Classic Vanilla batter, beating in a few drops of yellow food coloring after you add the vanilla.

Be careful not to overwhip the marshmallow batter; it will make folding in the cake mix a crazy, difficult mess.

Place a mesh sieve over the mixer bowl and sift about half the cake mix over the marshmallow batter. Use a spatula to gently fold it in and then sift and fold in the remainder of the cake mix. Fold in the rainbow sprinkles. Pour the marshmallow into the prepared pan, using an offset spatula to smooth it into the corners. Sift coating evenly and generously over top. Let it set for 6 hours in a cool, dry place.

Use a knife to loosen the marshmallow from the edges of the pan. Invert the slab onto a coating-dusted work surface and dust it with more coating. Cut into pieces and dip the sticky edges in more coating, patting off the excess. To decorate, combine the melted white chocolate and blue food coloring (or whatever color you like) and drizzle over each mallow, adding more sprinkles on top.

Try making huge slabs of these mallows in cake pans, stacking them, and decorating the whole thing like a birthday cake. It makes a great alternative cake for kids with food allergies or even a fun party centerpiece. For an awesomely messy party activity, lay out a bunch of icings and decors and let the kids go nuts.

MORE MALLOWS

Red Velvet Marshmallows: Swap out the yellow cake mix for red velvet. These are especially fun rolled in white chocolate sprinkles.

the mallowing

- 1 batch Classic Vanilla batter (page 16)
  Yellow gel food coloring*
- 1/4 cup yellow cake mix
- 2 tablespoons rainbow sprinkles
- 1/2 cup Classic Coating (page 8), plus more for dusting
- 6 ounces white chocolate, melted and cooled
  Blue gel food coloring

* A dab of yellow food coloring will make the mallows look even more cakelike, but blue and pink are fun, too.

MALLOW CONES

12 small cones

MAKE THE CONES: Position a rack near the center of the oven and preheat to 350°F. Line baking sheets with a silicone baking mat or lightly butter it. In a large bowl, whisk together the egg whites, sugar, butter, vanilla, and salt until smooth. Whisk in the flour. Scoop 4 two-teaspoon-sized spoonfuls onto the sheet. Use a small offset spatula or your fingertip to thinly smooth the batter into 4-inch rounds. Bake until the rounds are lightly golden all over and deeply golden at the edges, 8 to 9 minutes. Working quickly, roll each circle around a large pastry tip to form a cone and pinch the ends together. Rest them on a wire cooling rack; they will crisp as they cool. If the rounds become too firm before you've rolled them, pop the sheet back into the oven for 30 seconds to soften them. Repeat until all the batter is used. (If not using a silicone baking mat, butter the sheet pan before each batch.)

WHIP UP YOUR MARSHMALLOW BATTER, coloring and flavoring it as desired. Load the batter into a pastry bag fitted with a large round tip and pipe it into the cones. Decorate with sprinkles or other decors. Let set for 1 hour before serving. The longer the cones are stored, the softer they will become, so assemble as close to serving time as possible.

If preparing these for a party, the cones can be made a day ahead and stored in an airtight container. If they soften during storage, recrisp them in a 350°F oven for 5 minutes. Cool, dry days are best for making both the cones and the marshmallow.

the cones

- 2 large egg whites, at room temperature
- 6 tablespoons sugar
- 5 tablespoons unsalted butter, melted
- 1/2 teaspoon pure vanilla extract
- 1/8 teaspoon salt
- 1/3 cup all-purpose flour, sifted

the mallowing

- 1 batch marshmallow batter, any flavor*
  Gel food coloring, in any color
  Sprinkles or decors

* Any flavor of non-boozy marshmallow can be made into mallow cones. The cones on the opposite page are filled with pink-tinted Classic Vanilla (page 16).

IT'S A MARSHMALLOW WORLD: SWEET CRAFTY IDEAS

Flavor possibilities aside, marshmallows are versatile little gems. When the mallow has set, you can cut it into just about any shape or size. Kitchen-supply and baking stores offer a mind-boggling selection of cookie cutters that are perfect for creating shapes beyond the classic square.

A trusty piping bag is also a perfect tool for creating whimsical shapes. Experiment with different tips for marshmallows that fit any design you can dream up, from hearts and clouds to flowers and rosettes. They make pretty and unexpected cake decorations, just as you'd use fondant but a whole lot tastier.

The trick to piping mallow is to work quickly before the batter sets up and becomes too firm to pipe. If you find yourself in a sticky bind and are using a metal bowl, just scrape the mallow back down and heat the bowl briefly. You can set the bowl right on the stovetop over low heat for a few seconds, stirring all the while, until the batter has loosened. Then whip it again for a minute or two to get back to ideal mallow batter consistency. It can be messy, but it works!

Once you start experimenting with the many different ways to shape a mallow, you're sure to try all sorts of wacky marshmallowy crafts. Here are a few favorite fluffy puffy confectionery landscapes.

BLOOMING FLOWER GARDEN: Fill a clear glass vase about halfway with green sprinkles. Cure slabs of mallow in various colors and fruit flavors (such as Classic Vanilla, Concord Grape, Strawberry, Creamsicle, and Lemonade). Use cookie cutters to cut out flower shapes. Create multicolored daisies by removing the centers with a smaller circle cutter, dusting with coating, and replacing the circles in flowers of a different color. For stems, insert sturdy colored wire, long lollipop sticks, or thin wooden dowels (available at craft stores) into the flowers before arranging them in the vase.

MALLOWEEN GRAVEYARD: Cure Deeply Chocolate marshmallow batter in a shallow 9-by-13-inch baking pan (a quarter sheet pan works well). Sprinkle crushed chocolate wafers over the mallow for "dirt." Cut out Concord Grape gravestones and Pumpkin Spice jack-o-lanterns and pipe swirly mounds of Guimauve ghosts (follow the piping technique used for the Honeyed Apricot Marshmallows, page 39). Make "spider" cookies by piping blobs of marshmallow batter onto chocolate wafers, laying a few strips of licorice whips across, and sandwiching with more wafers, adding candy for eyes. Pipe melted chocolate details like ghost mouths and epitaphs to complete your spooky scene.

MARSHMALLOW SNOWMEN: Pipe various-sized mounds of Classic Vanilla or Guimauve batter onto a baking sheet dusted with Classic Coating. Dust them liberally with white sprinkles or coarse, sparkling white sanding sugar, or leave them bare. Fit the cured pieces onto lollipop sticks, stacking three mounds to resemble a little snowman. If you haven't sprinkled the marshmallow, coat the whole lot in melted white chocolate before adding candies and other decors.

MINI MALLOW WEDDING-CAKE FAVORS: Cut slabs of mallow in circles of three different sizes. Use melted white chocolate as glue and stack the circles like a wedding cake. Decorate with dots of royal icing, dragées, and shimmering cake dust. And speaking of adorable party favors, how about little bags of sweet, fluffy puffs, tied with cute ribbon, for bridal- and baby-shower favors? Use themed cookie cutters to cut marshmallow made with corresponding party colors and watch your guests ooh and ahh. (Marshmallow baby booties? So cute.)

MALLOW CHICKS: They're a classic and couldn't be simpler, just a piping technique with a bit of panache. Generously coat a baking sheet with colored sugar. Load Classic Vanilla or Guimauve batter into a large pastry bag fitted with a large round tip. Pipe a sort of vertical S curve, releasing pressure on the bag as you get about halfway through the curve, creating a face and beak. Coat generously with more colored sugar and let set. Pipe on dots of melted chocolate for your little peep's peepers.

FLUFFY, PUFFY DESSERTS

Sticky, Gooey Treats Made with Mallow

Now that you have a handle on whipping up marshmallows that are perfect for eating out of hand, let's take it to the next level and use our mad mallowing skills for some seriously awesome desserts. A basic marshmallow batter is the foundation for so many treats we all know and love. Depending on how you work with it and what you add, the result can serve as a topping, a frosting, a filling, a delightfully bouncy texture, even a delicious binder. Not to mention the ultimate guilty pleasure: handfuls of mallows bobbing in decadent drinkable desserts.

AMBROSIA CAKE

1 10-inch 3-layer cake

MAKE THE CAKE BATTER: Preheat the oven to 350°F. Coat a 10-inch tube pan with cooking spray. Into a medium bowl, sift the flour, baking powder, and salt. Heat the milk in the microwave on high power for 1 minute; then stir in the vanilla. In the bowl of an electric mixer fitted with the paddle attachment, beat the egg yolks with ¾ cup of the sugar until doubled in volume, about 3 minutes. Reduce speed to low and add the milk mixture. Gradually stir in the flour mixture.

Beat the egg whites on medium-high speed with an electric mixer fitted with the whisk attachment until soft peaks form, about 2 to 3 minutes. Gradually add the remaining ¼ cup sugar and beat until it holds stiff, glossy peaks, about 1 minute more.

Fold one-third of the egg whites into the yolk mixture, to lighten it; then fold in the remaining whites. When just a few streaks of egg white remain in the batter, gently fold in the pineapple, oranges, and cherries in two batches. Pour the batter into the prepared pan. Bake until the cake is a deep golden brown and a cake tester comes out clean, 45 to 50 minutes. Invert the cake pan onto a wire rack to cool completely in the pan, at least 1 hour.

This behemoth of a celebration cake is a bit of a project, but it's a showstopper and absolutely worth it. If necessary, the cake can be made a day ahead (cooled completely and wrapped well in plastic wrap), but make the frosting and assemble the cake on the day of serving for optimum fluff factor.

Continued...

THE CAKE BATTER

- 1 cup all-purpose flour
- 1 ½ teaspoons baking powder
- ½ teaspoon salt
- ⅓ cup milk
- 1 teaspoon pure vanilla extract
- 5 large eggs, separated, at room temperature
- 1 cup sugar, divided
- 1 (8-ounce) can crushed pineapple packed in juice, well-drained and patted dry
- 1 (11-ounce) can mandarin oranges in light syrup, well-drained and patted dry
- ⅓ cup (3 ounces) maraschino cherries, chopped and patted dry

WHISK TOGETHER the gelatin and water in a small bowl and let soften for 5 to 10 minutes.

MAKE THE MERINGUE FLUFF: Place the egg whites and cream of tartar in the clean bowl of an electric mixer fitted with the whisk attachment. Whip on high speed until firm peaks form. Stop the mixer.

STIR TOGETHER the sugar, corn syrup, water, and salt in a small saucepan over high heat. Boil, stirring occasionally, until it reaches 230°F.

To prep for the mallowing: Toast the pecans and coconut by tossing them together on a small baking sheet and baking in a 350°F oven until golden, about 10 minutes; stir frequently to prevent burning.

WHEN THE SYRUP reaches 230°F, scrape the gelatin into it and whisk until it melts, about 15 seconds. Set the mixer speed to medium and slowly pour syrup into the meringue fluff. Increase the speed to high and beat until the frosting is tripled in size and the bowl is cool to the touch, 7 to 8 minutes. Beat in the vanilla and almond extracts. Fold in the toasted coconut and pecan mixture, reserving ¼ cup for garnish.

Use a long serrated knife to slice the cake into three layers. Place one layer cut side up on a serving platter. Dollop a third of the frosting and spread evenly, leaving a ½-inch border. Lightly press the second layer on top of the first. Repeat with another third of the frosting and the last cake layer. Cover the cake with the remaining frosting, swirling it fancifully with a spatula or spoon. Sprinkle with the reserved ¼ cup toasted coconut and pecan mixture and garnish with maraschino cherries. Let the marshmallow set for 30 minutes before serving.

THE MARSHMALLOW FROSTING

the bloom
- 4 teaspoons unflavored powdered gelatin
- ¼ cup cold water

the meringue fluff
- 6 large egg whites, at room temperature
- ½ teaspoon cream of tartar

the syrup
- 1 cup sugar
- ½ cup light corn syrup
- ¼ cup water
- ¼ teaspoon salt

the mallowing
- 2 teaspoons pure vanilla extract
- ¾ teaspoon pure almond extract
- 1 cup sweetened shredded coconut, toasted
- ¾ cup chopped pecans, toasted
- Whole maraschino cherries, for garnish

LEMON DREAM WHOOPIE PIES

16 3-inch pies

Position oven racks in the upper and lower thirds of the oven and preheat to 350°F. Line 2 baking sheets with parchment paper.

MAKE THE CAKES: Sift together the flour, baking powder, baking soda, and salt in a medium bowl. In a small bowl, whisk together the milk, lemon juice, and vanilla. In the bowl of an electric mixer fitted with the paddle attachment, beat the butter, sugars, and lemon zest on medium speed until light and fluffy, about 2 minutes. Beat in the eggs one at a time. Reduce the speed to low and add the flour mixture and milk mixture in three alternating additions. When only a few streaks of flour remain, fold in the white chocolate chips by hand. Using a 2-tablespoon-sized ice-cream scoop or 2 spoons, place the batter 3 inches apart onto the prepared baking sheets. Bake until the cakes spring back when touched lightly, about 15 minutes; rotate the baking sheets from front to back and top to bottom halfway through baking. Transfer the sheets of parchment to cooling racks and let the cakes cool completely. Repeat with remaining batter.

WHILE THE CAKES ARE COOLING, place the butter in the bowl of an electric mixer fitted with the paddle attachment; beat until smooth and creamy. Beat in the marshmallow crème, followed by the confectioners' sugar, lemon extract, and yellow food coloring. Refrigerate the filling for at least 15 minutes. Load the filling into a pastry bag and generously pipe it onto half the cakes, sandwiching them with the other halves. Serve immediately.

See photo, page 78. Change up the flavor of these whoopies by omitting the lemon zest in the cakes and adding different extracts or oils to the cakes and filling.

the lemon cakes

- 2 ¼ cups all-purpose flour
- 1 teaspoon baking powder
- ½ teaspoon baking soda
- ½ teaspoon salt
- ½ cup milk
- ¼ cup lemon juice
- 1 teaspoon pure vanilla extract
- ½ cup (1 stick) unsalted butter, at room temperature
- ½ cup granulated sugar
- ½ cup light brown sugar
- 1 tablespoon lemon zest
- 2 large eggs, at room temperature
- ⅔ cup white chocolate chips

the mallow filling

- ½ cup (1 stick) unsalted butter, at cool room temperature
- 1 ½ cups Homemade Marshmallow Crème (page 26)
- 1 cup confectioners' sugar
- ½ teaspoon lemon extract
  Yellow gel food coloring

S'MORES CUPCAKES

1 dozen cupcakes

Preheat oven to 350°F. Line a 12-cup muffin tin with paper liners.

MAKE THE CRUST: Place graham crackers, sugar, and salt in the bowl of a food processor. Grind until fine. With the processor running, pour in the melted butter and mix until the crumbs are evenly moistened, resembling wet sand. Divide the crumb mixture evenly among the muffin tins, about 1 ½ tablespoons per well. Using your fingertips, firmly press each portion of crumb mixture, compacting it into an even layer. Bake until crusts are firm and slightly golden, about 7 minutes. Cool in tins on a wire rack; leave the oven on.

MAKE THE CAKES: Sift together the flour, sugar, cocoa, baking soda, baking powder, and salt in the bowl of an electric mixer. In a medium bowl, whisk together the egg, coffee, buttermilk, oil, and vanilla. Starting with the mixer on low speed, mix the dry ingredients for 30 seconds; slowly pour in the wet ingredients. Increase the speed to medium and beat for 2 minutes. Divide the batter evenly among the muffin tins, pouring it on top of the baked crusts; the cups should be no more than three-quarters full. Bake until the tops of the cupcakes spring back when touched lightly, 22 to 25 minutes. Set on a wire rack to cool.

This chocolate cake is the sort that will have everyone asking you for the recipe. The combination of coffee and buttermilk gives spectacular depth and richness to the chocolate flavor, and the texture is divine—dense, tender, and moist all at once.

Continued...

THE CHOCOLATE GRAHAM
CRACKER CUPCAKES

the crust

3	ounces graham cracker crumbs*
2	tablespoons sugar
⅛	teaspoon salt
3	tablespoons unsalted butter, melted

the cakes

¾	cup all-purpose flour
¾	cup sugar
6	tablespoons dark unsweetened cocoa powder
¾	teaspoon baking soda
½	teaspoon baking powder
¼	teaspoon salt
1	large egg
6	tablespoons strong brewed coffee
6	tablespoons buttermilk
2	tablespoons canola oil
½	teaspoon pure vanilla extract

* About 6 full sheets store-bought crackers, or see page 27 for Homemade Graham Cracker recipes.

S'MORES CUPCAKES, CONT.

WHISK TOGETHER the gelatin and cold water. Let soften for 5 minutes.

PLACE THE EGG WHITES and cream of tartar in the bowl of an electric mixer fitted with the whisk attachment. Beat on high speed until soft peaks form, 2 to 3 minutes. Stop the mixer.

STIR TOGETHER the sugar, corn syrup, water, and salt in a medium saucepan over high heat. Boil, stirring occasionally, until the temperature reaches 230°F.

WHEN THE SYRUP reaches 230°F, quickly whisk in the gelatin. Set the mixer to medium speed and carefully drizzle a few tablespoons of syrup into the egg whites to warm them and avoid scrambling them. Repeat 2 or 3 more times with a few more drizzles and then pour in the rest of the syrup. Beat on high speed until the frosting is tripled in size, 7 to 8 minutes. Beat in the vanilla extract.

Load the icing into a pastry bag fitted with a large tip. Pipe generous swirls of frosting on each cupcake or dollop it on with a spatula. Toast lightly with a kitchen torch. Alternatively, you can place small batches of cupcakes on a baking sheet and pop them under a broiler, watching closely to prevent burning and melting.

These cupcakes are best eaten the day they are made. If necessary, you can bake the cakes a day ahead and then make, pipe, and toast the frosting the day you're going to serve them.

THE TOASTED MARSHMALLOW FROSTING

the bloom
- 2 teaspoons unflavored powered gelatin
- 2 tablespoons cold water

the fluff
- 6 large egg whites, at room temperature
- ¼ teaspoon cream of tartar

the syrup
- 1 cup sugar
- ½ cup light corn syrup
- ¼ cup water
- ¼ teaspoon salt

the mallowing
- 2 teaspoons pure vanilla extract

CHOCOLATE-MARSHMALLOW ROULADE

1 rolled cake, serves 10

MAKE THE CAKE: Position a rack in the center of the oven and preheat to 350°F. Line a 12-by-17-by-1-inch baking sheet with parchment paper or silicone baking mats (not waxed paper) and coat with cooking spray. Place the chocolate and butter in a medium heatproof bowl. Melt in the microwave, with 30-second bursts of high power, stirring well after each interval.

Sift together the flour, cocoa, and baking soda in a medium bowl. In the bowl of an electric mixer fitted with the paddle attachment, beat the eggs and sugar on medium-high speed until tripled in volume, about 5 minutes. Reduce the speed to low and stir in the cooled chocolate mixture. Stir in the dry ingredients and coffee in three alternating additions. Pour the batter into the prepared pan. Bake for 15 minutes, or until cake springs back when touched lightly. Invert it onto a clean tea towel covered with a clean sheet of parchment. Peel back the parchment from the cake. Carefully roll the warm cake and transfer it to a wire rack to cool completely.

BEAT TOGETHER the marshmallow crème and butter until just combined. Slowly unroll the cooled cake. Spread the filling evenly over top, leaving a 1-inch border on all sides. Reroll the cake, leaving behind the parchment paper. Gently slide both hands underneath the rolled cake and quickly transfer it to a serving platter. Refrigerate while you prepare the glaze.

COMBINE THE CHOCOLATE and cream in a heatproof bowl. Melt in the microwave, with 30-second bursts of medium power, stirring well after each interval. To finish, tuck clean strips of parchment paper under the edges of the cake to protect the plate from smears. Cover the cake completely with glaze. Refrigerate to just set the glaze; remove parchment before serving.

Essentially what you're making is a three-pound Ho-Ho. It's glorious! It's the sort of mind-blowing thing that is the stuff of legends.

the cake
- 6 ounces bittersweet chocolate, chopped (60% to 70% cacao)
- 6 tablespoons unsalted butter
- 1 cup flour, divided
- 3 tablespoons dark unsweetened cocoa powder
- ½ teaspoon baking soda
- 4 large eggs
- 1 cup granulated sugar
- ¾ cup strong brewed coffee

the mallow filling
- 1 ½ cups Homemade Marshmallow Crème (page 26)
- ½ cup (1 stick) unsalted butter, at cool room temperature

the chocolate glaze
- 6 ounces bittersweet chocolate, chopped (60% to 70% cacao)
- 6 ounces heavy cream

MINTY MALLOW COOKIE SANDWICHES

2 dozen small sandwiches, or 8 to 10 large ones

◆ **PLACE HALF** the wafers bottom side up on a large baking pan.

◆ **WHIP UP A BATCH** of Classic Vanilla batter, adding the peppermint extract and green food coloring with the vanilla in the last minute of beating. Transfer the batter to a pastry bag fitted with a large round tip. Pipe generous mounds of marshmallow onto each cookie. Sandwich the mounds with the remaining wafers.

Melt the chocolate chips in a heatproof bowl over a double boiler or in the microwave, with 30-second bursts of high power, stirring well after each interval. Transfer the melted chocolate to a small pastry bag fitted with a small round tip (or into a sandwich bag, using kitchen scissors to snip the tip off one corner). Generously and artfully drizzle each cookie sandwich with the chocolate. Refrigerate until the chocolate is firm, about 10 to 15 minutes, before serving.

For smaller sandwiches, use chocolate wafer cookies. To make bigger ones like those pictured at right, try Italian pizelles (available at specialty grocers).

◆ the wafers
> 1 (9-ounce) package thin, crisp chocolate wafers* or Italian pizelles

◆ the mallowing
> ½ batch Classic Vanilla batter
> ½ teaspoon peppermint extract
> Green gel food coloring
> 8 ounces bittersweet chocolate chips

* Nabisco's Famous Chocolate Wafers are a classic and a great choice for this recipe.

WHITE CHOCOLATE MALT CRISPY RICE TREATS

2 dozen treats

● **WHIP UP A BATCH** of Classic Vanilla Marshmallows, and let cure at least 8 hours. Cut the marshmallow slab in half. Cut one half in a few large pieces and the remaining half into rough mini marshmallows (about ½-inch cubes). Toss the mini mallows in a bit of Classic Coating (page 8) or plain cornstarch to prevent sticking; dust off the excess. Lightly coat an 8-by-8-inch baking pan with cooking spray.

◆ **IN A LARGE, HEAVY-BOTTOMED POT,** melt the butter over medium-low heat. Add the large marshmallows and stir until almost melted. Toss in the chopped white chocolate and stir until melted and smooth. Blend in the malted milk powder and salt. Stir in the crisp rice cereal until evenly coated. Stir in the mini mallows and quickly and evenly press the mixture into the prepared pan. Let set at room temperature for 1 hour before cutting into bars.

Melt the remaining 1 ½ ounces of white chocolate in a small bowl and artfully drizzle a bit over each treat. Let the chocolate set for 15 minutes before serving.

MANIPULATING YOUR MALLOW

Homemade mallows are quite a bit softer and contain more moisture than their commercial counterparts. Although this makes them all the more delicious, they tend to soften things like cereal or popcorn. The trick to making homemade mallows work in these recipes is to reduce the water in the Bloom stage, cook the sugar syrup to a higher temperature (250°F instead of 240°F), and dry the mallow a little longer. The result is a firmer, drier marshmallow.

● the mallowing

   1 batch Classic Vanilla Marshmallows (page 16)*

◆ the crispy rice treats

   4 tablespoons unsalted butter

   4 ounces chopped white chocolate

  ½ cup plain malted milk powder*

  ¼ teaspoon salt

   6 cups crisp rice cereal

1 ½ ounces white chocolate, for drizzling (optional)

* For this recipe, reduce the water in the Bloom stage to ⅓ cup and cook the syrup to 250°F. Let set for at least 8 hours.

* This can be found near the hot cocoa or ice-cream fixings in supermarkets.

BALLPARK POPCORN BALLS

1 dozen balls

◆ **WHIP UP A BATCH** of Classic Vanilla Marshmallows and let cure for at least 8 hours. Divide the marshmallow slab into thirds. Cut one-third into a few large pieces and the remaining two-thirds into rough mini marshmallows (about ½-inch cubes). Toss the mini mallows in a bit of Classic Coating (page 8) or plain cornstarch to prevent sticking; dust off the excess.

◆ **MAKE THE POPCORN MIX:** Pour the vegetable oil into a large heavy-bottomed pot (such as a Dutch oven) over high heat. Toss in a few kernels of unpopped popcorn and cover the pot. When all the kernels have popped, add the rest and cover. Shake the pot occasionally while the corn is popping and remove it from the heat when the popping slows to 3 seconds between pops. Season lightly with salt and transfer to a large mixing bowl, removing unpopped kernels. You should have 15 to 16 cups of popped corn. Add the peanuts and pretzel pieces to the mixing bowl.

If you prefer to use microwave popcorn, just make sure you have 15 to 16 cups' worth.

Wipe out the pot and place it on the stove over low heat. Drop in the butter and large marshmallow pieces, stirring until melted. Remove the pot from the heat and add the popcorn mixture, tossing to coat. Stir in the mini mallows. If adding chocolate chips, let the mixture cool a bit before stirring them in.

Coat your clean hands generously with cooking spray and press the mixture into 12 balls. (You may need to wash your hands and respray them once or twice to make working with the mixture easier.) Let the popcorn balls firm up at room temperature for 20 minutes before serving.

Wrapped up, these make awesome party favors or tailgate treats. Cut squares of cellophane, roll up each ball individually, and cinch and tie the ends with ribbon or twist ties, like a giant piece of candy.

◆ **the mallowing**
- 1 batch Classic Vanilla Marshmallows (page 16)*

◆ **the popcorn mix**
- ¼ cup vegetable oil
- ½ cup unpopped popcorn kernels
- Salt
- 1 cup honey-roasted peanuts
- 2 cups thin pretzel sticks, broken into ½-inch pieces
- 1 tablespoon unsalted butter
- ½ cup mini semi-sweet chocolate chips (optional)

* For this recipe, reduce the water in the Bloom stage to ⅓ cup and cook the syrup to 250°F. Let set for at least 8 hours. See "Manipulating Your Mallow" on the previous page.

BLONDE ROCKY ROAD

About 2 dozen 1 ½ inch squares

Line an 8-by-8-inch baking pan with a large sheet of aluminum foil, pressing it neatly into the corners.

In a large, microwave-safe bowl, combine the butterscotch chips, peanut butter, and butter. Microwave on 50% power for about 3 minutes. Stop to stir well. Place back in the microwave for 1 minute and 30 seconds on 50% power and stop to stir again—it should be smooth after a bit more stirring. If not, give it a couple more 30-second bursts of high power and stir until smooth.

Stir in the vanilla and salt. Stir in 2 cups of the marshmallows and ½ cup of the peanuts. Turn the mixture into the prepared pan and smooth with a spatula. Sprinkle the remaining marshmallows and peanuts evenly over the top and press lightly into the candy with your palms. Chill until set, about 15 minutes in the freezer or 1 hour in the refrigerator.

Remove the candy slab from the pan and cut it into 1½-inch squares. Store in an airtight container in the refrigerator for up to 1 week.

1   12-ounce bag butterscotch chips

½   cup creamy peanut butter*

½   cup (1 stick) unsalted butter, cut into tablespoon-size pieces

½   teaspoon pure vanilla extract

⅛   teaspoon salt

2 ½   cups Homemade Mini Marshmallows (page 17), divided

¾   cup salted peanuts, divided

* Opt for smooth commercial peanut butter for a melt-in-your mouth texture.

DESSERTS MADE DRINKABLE

Warm steaming mugs of something sweet and decadent beg for a handful (or three) of homemade mallows. It's almost desserty enough to make you forget about cake. Almost. Here's a few drinkable desserts, along with excellent marshmallow-pairing suggestions.

MALTED WHITE HOT CHOCOLATE
Serves 2

- 1 cup whole milk
- 1 cup half-and-half
- 3 ounces good-quality white bar chocolate, chopped*
- 1/8 teaspoon salt
- 1/4 cup plain malted milk powder
- 3/4 teaspoon pure vanilla extract
  Freshly grated nutmeg, for garnish (optional)

*I recommend bar chocolate over chips. In some recipes, it doesn't matter, but bar chocolate makes this drink noticeably silkier and more lush.

Combine the milk, half-and-half, white chocolate, and salt in a medium saucepan. Stir over medium-low heat until the chocolate is completely melted and the mixture is just becoming hot to the touch. Transfer to a blender and add the malted milk powder. Cover tightly and blend for 60 seconds. Return the mixture to the saucepan and reheat until hot, stirring in the vanilla. Serve immediately, topped with a smattering of nutmeg.

Recommended Mallow Pairings: Classic Vanilla, Chocolate Filled, Honeyed Apricot, Buttered Rum, Mallows in the Raw

ULTIMATE HOT CHOCOLATE
Serves 2

- 1 3/4 cups whole milk
- 1/4 cup half-and-half
- 1/4 cup light brown sugar, firmly packed
- 2 ounces bittersweet chocolate, chopped (60% to 70% cacao)
- 2 tablespoons dark unsweetened cocoa powder
- 1/4 teaspoon instant espresso powder
- 1/8 teaspoon salt
- 1/2 teaspoon pure vanilla extract

Combine the milk, half-and-half, brown sugar, chocolate, cocoa, espresso powder, and salt in a medium saucepan. Whisk to blend over medium heat. When the chocolate is melted and the mixture is just hot to the touch, transfer it to a blender. Cover tightly and blend for 60 seconds. Return mixture to the saucepan over medium heat and stir in the vanilla. Reheat until hot but not boiling. Serve immediately.

Recommended Mallow Pairings: Classic Vanilla, Chocolate Malt, Chocolate-Peppermint, Crème de Menthe, Sea Salt Caramel Swirl, Fluffernutter